Christian
Spiritual
Formation
in the Church and
Classroom

SUSANNE JOHNSON

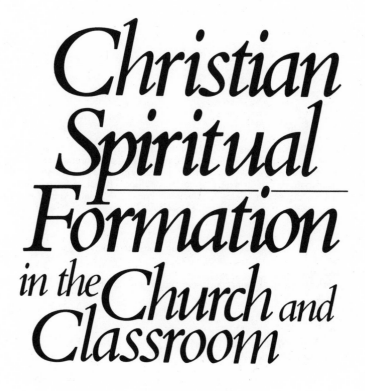

Christian Spiritual Formation

in the Church and Classroom

ABINGDON PRESS

Nashville

Christian Spiritual Formation in the Church and Classroom

Copyright © 1989 by Abingdon Press

This book is printed on acid-free paper.

Johnson, Susanne.
    Christian spiritual formation in the church and classroom / Susanne Johnson.
    p. cm.
    Bibliography: p.

    ISBN 0-687-07590-4 (alk. paper)
    1. Christian education—Philosophy. 2. Spirituality. I. Title.
    BV1464.j64 1989
    268'. 804—dc20   89-31939
                                                        CIP

MANUFACTURED BY THE PARTHENON PRESS AT
NASHVILLE, TENNESSEE, UNITED STATES OF AMERICA

To My Parents

Philippians 1:3

CONTENTS

Introduction.. 11

1. Drinking from Our Own Wells: An
   Introduction... 15

   Basic Claims 19; Rebirth of Images 22; Participation as
   Paradigm 24

2. Drinking from Other Wells: A Partial Critique..30

   The Rise of Psycho-Culture 30; The Triumph of Ethical
   Egoism 33; The Triumph of the Therapeutic 35; The
   Triumph of Individualism 38; The Triumph of Feminist
   Ideology 39

3. Participation: Theological Foundations................ 43

   Participating in the Realm of God 43

4. Participation: Practical Foundations..................... 55

   Worship: A Pattern for Discipline 62

5. Participation: Church as Context............................ 70

The Church as the People of God 70; The Church as
Event 73; The Church in the Spirit 74; The Church:
Redemptive? 75; The Church as the Family of God 81;
The Ecclesial Shape of Spirituality 85

6. Participation: Story as Content............................. 87

We Are Storied People 87; Story: A Metaphor for Reality
88; Scripture and Tradition: A Vast Story! 89; Listening
to Stories 90; Christian Story and Christian Education 91;
We Read the Story 93; The Story Reads Us 95;
Guidelines to Reading 99

7. Christian Spiritual Formation............................. 103

The Dominance of Developmentalism 105; Psychological
Approaches to Human Change and Growth 106; Ego, Self,
Christian Self 108; Christian Character and Christian
Education 111; Formation and Transformation 117

8. Church: An Ecology of Spiritual Care and
   Formation.. 121

Environment of Grace 122; General Guidance: What the
Church Is and Does 124; Group Guidance 126;
One-to-One Guidance 129; Hidden Guidance 132

9. Christian Education for Formation..................... 136

Teaching: Science or Art? 140; Christian Education: The
Dynamic Processes 143; The Church Instructs 146; The
Church Engages in Praxis 149

Epilogue.. 156

Notes... 161

Christian Spiritual Formation
in the Church and Classroom

Introduction

I

Yet another book on spirituality? Yes, but not another how-to book! This work takes up a discussion of the meaning of spirituality for the American Protestant church today. I attempt to get hold of some "weasel words" currently popular in churches and seminaries: spirituality, formation, spiritual discipline and direction. The book is part of an ongoing quest occurring throughout the churches to recover spiritual direction (care of souls) as a renewed motive for Christian ministry.

There is a tremendous flurry of interest in spirituality in the churches, in the seminaries, and in popular American culture. Never before have there been so many books published, so many conferences, consultations, seminary courses, workshops, cassette tapes, retreats, how-to manuals, curriculum resources, and other activities devoted to drawing persons into spirituality. Some believe the Christian church to be caught up in one of those great moments of spiritual quickening that from time to time in its pilgrimage serves to renew its very foundations. Interest in spirituality has reached a new pitch in contemporary culture, presenting a challenge to the church, however, to discern the authentic from the bogus. The cultural captivity of religion in America makes this a particularly difficult task.

The credibility of the so-called new spirituality is a

persistent issue. Many persons in the churches and seminaries are reluctant to embrace the notion of spirituality. There are too many peddlers of quick-fix spirituality, and too few writers helping the church think critically about it.

What troubles me about the new spiritual awakening is the seemingly widespread revival of "spirituality without Christianity," a phenomenon as evident in the church as in the culture. The American religious milieu has witnessed an unprecedented influx of individuals into esoteric cults and Eastern spiritual psychologies. At the same time, we have seen an alarming drop in church membership in mainline Protestant denominations. Membership in mainline churches in the United States has been on a steady, precipitous decline for several decades. The question pressing the church is not so much whether our children will have spirituality but whether Christianity will have our children![1]

Part of our problem today is that the word "spirituality" itself—though a notion with roots deep in Christian history—is quite new in the Protestant lexicon.[2] The word is used so loosely in the literature that it is difficult to discern what it means. Spirituality has become cluttered with definitions. If the Christian church today is to recover authentic Christian spirituality, then we must clarify our terminology. We especially need to reclaim our biblical-historical roots. In this book I shall seek in particular to recover a biblical and theological frame of reference for spirituality. New Testament spirituality is rooted in the Pauline moral sense of life lived under the pervasive influence of the Spirit of God. As Paul put it, we are to "walk in the Spirit." This entire book is based on the assumption of this moral sense.

II

Too much contemporary spirituality has lost its historical moorings. Modern Christians are largely content to swim in the warm stream of the immediate. Recasting an Old Testament image, Gustavo Gutierrez reminds us that spirituality in the life of the church can continue to exist only when it sends us back to our decisive sources. We must drink from our own wells (Prov. 5:15).[3] Don Saliers reminds us, in this respect, that Christian worship and spirituality must center in the common memory of those who gather about the font, the book, and the table.[4] Christians today, to a great extent, have taken on the name "Christian" without appropriating the Story, the living memory, that determines the meaning of the name they bear! Hence, they cannot see their lives in continuity with the redemptive history into which they have been adopted, namely, the whole biblical story of God's work "for us" through Israel and the life, death, and resurrection of Jesus Christ.[5]

This book, therefore, represents an attempt to assess and rethink the spirituality that dominates the churches of North America, and to move to a radical reappropriation of Christian spirituality based on biblical theological themes. The claim is made that the hermeneutical key to biblical spirituality is our participation in the creative and redemptive activity of God, symbolized as the Realm of God.

Spirituality as participation in God's work in the world carries us beyond the private zones of human existence to places we never before imagined. Our spirituality, when authentically Christian, establishes us in communion and solidarity with all that God creates and loves. In this light, all the spiritual disciplines become dangerous and daring exercises of collective hope for the New Creation.

III

Because I propose to view spiritual formation as the key organizing concept for Christian education, the structure of this book is designed to address some basic questions and categories of Christian educational theory. My overall intent is to explore spiritual formation as the decisive guiding image for educational ministry in the church.

Chapters 1 and 2 present the basic problem that the book seeks to redress. Chapters 3 through 6 present the foundations for an alternative approach, with chapters 3 and 4 presenting theological and practical foundations respectively, chapter 5 looking at the church as the context of formation, and chapter 6 exploring Christian Story as the content of formation. Chapter 7, "Christian Spiritual Formation," lays out the heart of the proposal. Chapter 8 views the church as an ecology of spiritual formation and guidance, and chapter 9 suggests that the three deliberate and sustained processes for Christian spiritual formation are worship, praxis, and instruction.

1

Drinking from Our Own Wells:
An Introduction

Signs posted everywhere in our society whisper the deep yearning of modern men and women for a sense of connectedness with the Sacred. There is an interest, unprecedented in modern times, in spiritual experience and in prayer and meditation, not only in America but also across the globe.

Put another way, it is apparent that modern men and women long desperately for a soul, for spiritual self-transcendence. Don Marquis claimed that you don't have to have a soul unless you really want one.[1] So very many persons want their souls, but do not know how to find them! They yearn to know God and what God wants of them but do not know where to turn for guidance.

The search for spiritual self-transcendence is a primal response wrung from human beings in the face of finitude, in the midst of the tragic, in the pathos of human suffering and pain. For most men and women, it is the occasion of real difficulty that prompts the deepest expression, however clumsy and naïve, of their spirituality. The grim phone call in the night, after which life is never quite the same, compels a man or woman to want to know God in the deepest possible way.

Our most poignant prayers are cries wrung from us in the face of suffering occasioned by the death of family and friends, by the specter of death crouched on our own chest, by the loneliness and struggle of daily survival, by events that stretch us beyond the limits of our moral insight and our powers of emotional endurance, by the realization that evil always lurks around the corner.

We want to be spiritual people, we want to know God, but often we do not know how. We are not entirely sure what to make of such notions as spirituality, transformation, or conversion. We are turned off by one televangelist yet tantalized by the promising message of another. We are surrounded by a spate of self-help books in spiritual psychology but do not know whether to dig in. From the glitz of religious talk shows, we hear stories of dramatic conversions but then become suspicious of sham. We wistfully toy with techniques that relax us and that promise us a life abundant with the blessings of health, wealth, and a happy home. Yet, in the end, we still find ourselves straining for a deeper sense of spiritual assurance, inner peace, and unqualified grace.

We hear the diagnosis from some theologians, to the contrary, that modern Westerners are not drawn to spirituality and religious faith because they are now scientific, secular, and materialistic. According to popular diagnosis, contemporary Americans have acquired a critical scientific intellect and hence no longer can accept the supposed mythologies of Christianity. Jacques Ellul, however, estimates this to be a major diagnostic error.

Ellul reasons that if modern people have no authentic faith or spirituality, it is *not* because they are scientific, *not* because they have left the mentality of myth behind, *not* because they are materialistic. It is because they are so naïve and gullible, ready to take up with the latest fashion, fad, or myth. Modern individuals, in fact, flock precisely to the things that are most mythical, ecstatic, and apocalyptic, perceives Ellul.[2] Witness Ramtha adherents! Witness Shirley McLain!

Ellul is not at all flattering about us! Yet the fact remains that while we do yearn deeply to be connected with the Sacred, not the secular, we have trouble distinguishing between false gods and God, between Christian hope and mere credulity, between spiritual discipline and spiritual charlantanry, between spiritual depth and emotional froth, between Christian witness and civil religion.

Although America is an officially religious ("one nation under God") and optimistic society, as Douglas Hall points out, we in fact live in an age of diminished corporate hope and optimism.[3] We do not actually believe that anything good can collectively come out of the human race, out of politics or government or international relations or educational institutions, or the public domain. Hence, many Americans retreat into the private world of self and there become pathologically preoccupied with their own personal growth. The deep human need to hope in something is diverted from the public to the private, leading, among other things, to an intensely isolationist spirituality. My greatest concern is that the so-called new spirituality really does not set persons free *from* narcissism and free *for* others, including themselves. Instead, within contemporary culture, it tends to compound the tendency to self-preoccupation and rampant individualism.

The unfortunate situation of many modern men and women is that they do not know how to emerge from the abyss of self-absorption to address their deep spiritual yearnings. Because they do not know how to name or to satisfy their spiritual hunger, they feed themselves indiscriminately. Too many modern individuals, observes Don Browning, are content to live on scraps. Starving people will settle for anything! But as Fred Craddock puts it, it is not simply in chewing but in chewing good food that people are nourished.[4]

The galloping gullibility to which Ellul alludes constitutes one of the greatest challenges to teaching and to spiritual direction in the church today. So many Christians do not know the distinction between the Christian Story and the many other stories that orient them spiritually. Christian Story, modern psychologies, and civil religion have quite different things to say about the world. Yet many believers confuse the critical differences as they move about in their workaday worlds.

If we have no convictions or if they are weakly held, culture will supply them for us. As Eugene Rosenstock-Huessey says, the human heart "either falls in love with somebody or something, or it falls ill. It can never go unoccupied."[5] We will fasten onto one interpretation of life or another because we cannot bear up under the thought that we are adrift in an absurd and random world. Nor can we bear the thought that God plays dice with the universe. We need a Story that truthfully renders to us the shape of the world and that equips us spiritually and morally to live in it.

The symbols of the Christian faith deny that life is unendurable and meaningless. They do not deny that life hurts. They permit us to admit that we are subject to chance, to necessity, to transiency, but to deny that we are castaways in a pointless world. These symbols give us the courage and the skill to negotiate life as it really is. It is through spiritual guidance and the practice of discipline that the church helps believers participate in the divine reality to which these symbols point.

Fortunately, spiritual direction (the care and cure of souls, whatever we may want to call it!) has become a concern prominent in the contemporary ministry of the church. Spirituality and formation are no longer strangers to the concerns of modern believers and to the teaching ministry of the church. Yet the church remains in need of a closer look at how it may understand spiritual formation as the heart of its ministry. This book is intended as a critical examination of these issues, particularly in light of the teaching office of the Protestant church in America today.

BASIC CLAIMS

The exploration of spirituality and formation in the chapters that follow is based on several methodological considerations.

1. To begin with, it is not enough to go about the business of spirituality as though it were something generic. We must begin with the normative framework within which spirituality is to be understood and assessed. This book addresses itself to that framework. The themes of *participation* and *formation*, theologically and educationally understood, are the threads that provide conceptual continuity.

Spiritual formation simply is not intelligible apart from the communal context and faith tradition in which people are formed. How can we best understand this history and this community? What decisive Story is this community seeking to tell?[6] As H. R. Niebuhr reminds us, "when we become members of such a community of selves we adopt its past as our own and thereby are changed in our present existence."[7]

It is Christianity that creates *Christian* spirituality, and it is participation in Christianity that nourishes Christian spiritual formation. To grasp the nature of spiritual formation, when it is Christian, we must grasp the significance of taking on the name and identity of *Christian*.

2. Spirituality is not only a given. It is a reality that is learned. Unless one wants to be a spiritual orphan, there is a content and a grammar to spirituality that must be taught and learned, especially in the context of the local congregation. Christianity includes its own decisive logic of participation

and formation. The church not only *does* formation but also *is* a spiritually formative community. By its nature, it is an ecology of spiritual guidance and formation.

In this context, the Christian Scriptures and tradition, along with reason and experience, are decisive sources that evoke, shape, and sustain our spiritual existence as Christian believers.

3. Spiritual formation does not lie in Maslow's unending escalator to self-actualization. But it does involve an ongoing inner transformation. The primordial concern of spiritual formation is with the issue of *becoming*. What sort of person do I, do we, wish to become? By what story do we wish to be formed over the course of a lifetime? How shall we sponsor such becoming? What skills shall empower us in the journey of becoming?[8] These are all questions of Christian *vocation*. They transport us into concern for how the church equips Christians for their lifelong vocational calling.

4. The process of being changed is what Christians have called sanctification. It is what we mean today by the formation and shaping of Christian *character*. We do not simply develop through linear stages. Rather, our character is qualified in this direction or that, as our own life stories unfold under the impact of the Christian Story. Moreover, what is decisive in formation is not so much the dynamics but rather the direction of such processes. The central focus is upon the image and likeness—the truly human existence as revealed in Jesus Christ—into which individuals and communities are conformed by the Story.

5. Another claim is that when we talk about spiritual formation, we are really discoursing about *Christian formation*. I have grown immensely concerned that the way we talk about spiritual formation makes it sound like it as a "thing" apart from formation of Christian character. The impression is left that spirituality is something that can be understood

quite apart from becoming Christian in the first place. I argue that this is decidedly not the case.

Talk about spiritual formation transports us into concern with what it means for people to be formed as Christians over the course of a lifetime and how that happens. Our concern is not only with how a person becomes Christian but also with how one person helps another become Christian, and how we teach Christianity.

6. When we discourse about spiritual formation, our conversation must also be about the church. When we focus on the church, we are face to face with the mystery of being built into the household *(oikoumene)* of God. This refers to God's activity in the whole world and not simply to the churches. The fundamental theme of Ephesians is the gift of our participation in God's "plan for the fulness of time, to unite all things in him, things in heaven and things on earth" (Eph. 1:10). The shape of spirituality turns upon our freedom to participate in God's *oikonomia* (housekeeping or household management). To become Christian is, at its very heart, to be initiated into God's Realm.

A final thesis, broadly undergirding the entire discussion, is that there is no task more urgent than reorienting our ministry in spirituality, especially through recovering the offices of teaching and spiritual direction in the Protestant church. This will require liberal mainline churches to overcome their natural shyness about the exercise of authority. We must become clear that it is possible to teach with real authority without becoming authoritarian.

Going Beneath Tactics

Discussion of spiritual renewal in the church has been carried on mostly at the tactical level. This issues, of course, from an inchoate sense of optimism that something important is going on and that we ought quickly to jump on board. In this work, however, I wish to shift the discussion from the tactical level. This work will remain close to a conceptual level, attempting theological and theoretical clarification of spirituality, formation, discipline, and direction. This work, moreover, shifts the axis in spirituality away from the predominating psychological hermeneutic, described in chapter 2, to a more biblical-theological hermeneutic.

Understood from a Christian perspective, I propose that *spirituality is our self-transcendent capacity as human beings to recognize and to participate in God's creative and redemptive activity in all of creation.* This means, as we shall see throughout, that I advocate a spirituality that is both creation and redemption based. Their difference is far too overdrawn, if not outright caricatured, by certain writers today (cf. Matthew Fox).[9] The shape of God's redemptive work in the world is traditionally symbolized as kingdom of God, though feminist writers prefer equally biblical symbols such as New Creation, New Age, *basileia*, Realm of God, or "household of freedom."[10]

Spirituality, understood as actual participation in the Realm of God, is the key to recovering a biblical theological motive for Christian ministry. The process of initiating persons into the Realm of God links the teaching office of the church with its office of spiritual direction. Concern for overcoming the church's eclipse of spirituality, on the one hand, and of eschatology (God's Realm), on the other, is not entirely new to this work. Yet the time has come to bring these two perspectives together and to show how they yield insights relevant to the current malaise in Christian ministry.

REBIRTH OF IMAGES

Our contemporary milieu is marked by a widespread spiritual hunger, paralleled by a growing disenchantment with the institutional church, particularly mainline Protestantism. Unfortunately, we are thereby left with a far-reaching revival of "spirituality without Christianity." Ironically, this is evident as much in the churches as in culture itself.

Many feminists, for instance, in seeking to reclaim authentic spirituality, have disaffiliated themselves from the institutional church. Carol Ochs argues, in fact, that spirituality cannot be transformed unless women take seriously their own experience *only* and reject matters of authority, belief, doctrine, and ecclesial hierarchy.[11] The feminist response is to claim a specifically feminist spirituality. According to Susan Cady, this means to experience, to express, and to effect the radical interconnectedness of all creation, and the radical equality of all human beings.[12]

This vision is definitely not one gained from our experience in culture. It is gained, rather, from the fundamental witness of Christian Scriptures! Shining through the biblical witness, despite its patriarchy, is a vision of connectedness and mutuality as the shape of reality. Therefore, to experience, to express, and to effect this vision is to claim the ministry into which every Christian is ordained through baptism. We can see this clearly in the baptismal formula of Galatians 3:27-29 and the sublime witness of Ephesians 2:11-22.

The recovery of Christian spirituality, therefore, cannot come through a debunking of Scripture and tradition. How do we know ourselves to be sacred and inviolable children of God? How do we know that the exclusion of women and people of color is scandalous? From the radical message announced by Jesus. Where do we meet Jesus? Not through culture! He comes to us out of a social history, that is the faith community, that presents a vision counter to that of culture (though at times it seems co-opted to culture). Through the resources of the church, as well as through our own experience, we *do* meet Jesus, who authorizes us to say that

God wills the liberation rather than the oppression of women, people of color, the poor, and other marginalized persons.[13]

Images for spirituality today, thus, must be reborn with respect to the inclusive and humanizing vision witnessed to in the Christian Scriptures. Rejection of idolatrous images does not so much mean their destruction as their liberation. As Austin Farrer puts it, religion is transformed when its images are transformed. Such a transformation will determine the character and quality of spirituality.[14] Our call is not to reject the redemption imagery of Scriptures (in favor of creation images) but to see how, throughout the tradition, these images have possibly come to be distorted and disconnected from creation imagery.

Along with Ruether, I suggest that feminist and liberation theology must start with the church as the context for discussing questions of belief, action, ritual, and creed. In that context, we must deconstruct and reconstruct symbols and images of the human-God relationship. While feminist spirituality must repudiate the patriarchy of biblical religion, it must claim the underlying eschatological, prophetic base of the biblical story, precisely in order to raise questions about all forms of exclusivism. As Daniel Migliore insists, a crucial question of authentic Christian spirituality is not *whether* but *how* we read the Bible together.[15] The biblical narrative, in fact, contains a dangerous, subversive memory! It is a message not of subjugation, subordination, or subservience but of our freedom and mutuality as we participate together in the triune life of God.

PARTICIPATION AS PARADIGM

Participation, hence, is a key word in understanding Christian spiritual formation. Participation is a good old word in our tradition.[16] Associated originally with the Platonic and Neoplatonic tradition, the word has been key to creation theology as well as to thinking in the Western church. The idea of participation asserts that everything that exists participates already in the Everlasting Source of all life, or it would not exist at all.

Biblical writers who borrowed the term from the philosophical tradition changed its meaning. They built upon the Old Testament affirmation that we participate in God's reality through covenantal relationships. This is reflected in formulas that use "sharing," "partaking," and "participating." The Christian claim is that we participate in God's reality because God first participates in us.

The *imago Dei* is a creation metaphor for God's participation in us. It affirms that God created us with the capacity to recognize and to participate in all that God creates and loves. We are given a share in who God is and what God does! Whether or not we choose to accept our God-relatedness, we are grounded in the triune life of God. We manifest it, we share in it, we belong to it, we partake of it, we participate in it. The biblical Story is of a God who creates, who reconciles, who redeems, and in this, we have a share.

The *imago Dei* remains a permanent part of each one of us, even if this reality remains unappropriated. Though many people refuse, distort, and deny their fundamental nature, they can never finally destroy the image and likeness of God within them. Everyone has this gift. But we, being a stiff-necked and deceptive people, are prone to spend a lifetime obscuring, deforming, or denying it. To paraphrase Augustine, without God we are lumps of self-deception.

The *imago Dei* also affirms that we were created for community, because God's own self is expressed in terms of perfect mutuality, unity, and community. Our actual experience, though, is to the contrary. We are as apt to treat one another as threats, enemies, competitors, or strangers as gifts, neighbors, blessings, or fellow creatures. We use the metaphor of the Fall, in part, to confess that we try to do without one another and without God. To attempt this is to die, for we cannot live by bread alone. The Bible fears the death of abundant life far more than it fears sheer physical death. Through Christ and the Spirit we are given a new existence (new covenant) in the shape of the ecclesial community. The faith community itself is not the New Creation, but is to reflect the shape of God's work in bringing it about. Spirituality from the outset, then, is communal, while also very personal.

When we understand spirituality as participation in who God is and what God does, we maintain the preveniency of God's justifying and sanctifying grace. Spiritual discipline is not a program of self-improvement, not an ideal to be striven for, not a set of tasks to be accomplished. It is, rather, a way of posturing ourselves to receive God's work "for us" through Israel and in Jesus Christ.

When we construe spirituality as participation in God's *oikonomia* (housekeeping), then a spirituality cultivated in the private retreat of self is logically impossible. This theme affirms our interconnectedness and our indwelling with the whole of the created order. We are to look after the well-being of all creation, as well as one another, because it is, just as we are, sacred and inviolable. In the final analysis, says Harry Guntrip, the whole meaning of our human existence is found in our capacity for positive participation in our environment, beginning with mother and father and ending—with God.[17]

The Illusion of Participation

"There is no lack of information in a Christian land; something else is lacking, and is a something which the one [person] cannot directly communicate to the other," claimed Søren Kierkegaard.[18] Many people today say that what is obviously lacking is a rich and vital spirituality. My diagnosis is that the "something else" is best answered by the word "participation." What ails the church in the first instance is not that we are not "spiritual" enough. Starkly put, we are not Christian enough! I mean that we have not taken seriously the radical, countercultural, protracted process of Christian initiation.

One is not born but becomes a Christian (Tertullian). Kierkegaard suggested that it is easier to become a Christian when *not* one than it is to become a Christian when already one. Why would this be so? Because it is so easy to assume that we know how to participate in Christianity when in fact we may not.

We cannot assume that most church members know how. What ails much teaching and preaching, and spiritual guidance today, suggests Fred Craddock, is the flourishing illusion of participation where little or none actually exists.[19] Going to church is an important initial step, of course, yet it does not guarantee participation in Christian Story. The blessing of being nonchurched is that there is still the possibility of being confronted with a decision to participate. Once we are members, the decision has apparently been made.[20]

In the early church, persons seeking to join the household of faith were required to participate in a lengthy process (several years!) of training and instruction following their repentance and turn to Christ. No one presumed full incorporation into the body of Christ on the basis of the initial turn.

Becoming Christian was understood as a process of conversion and transformation that involved training in the skills required by the Christian Story, instruction in the sacred writings, assumption of a responsible role in the faith community, participation in its service and mission, intro-duction to the cloud of witnesses, the reshaping of ethical vision, and formation of ethical responsibilities. To take Christian initiation this seriously would hold revolutionary significance for spiritual renewal of the contemporary Protestant church!

SUMMARY

Within the contemporary church, there seems to be more fuss about spiritual formation than Christian formation. More people are, unfortunately, falling in love with spirituality than with God and neighbor. Believers turn to indiscriminate spirituality when they no longer remember their common story and how to negotiate its costly choices, its unexpected twists and turns, its surprises and gifts. Renewal of spirituality has always at heart been a call to renewed Christianity!

The real question for the church, therefore, is not *whether* we shall take up the task of formation but rather *how* we shall shape this ministry. This depends upon the extent to which we are aware that spirituality is at heart a matter of Christian formation. Christian formation, in turn, rests upon our careful attention to initiating believers into the Realm of God. The logic and grammar of Christian existence require that we reclaim the practices of spiritual discipline and direction. One cannot become Christian without learning to pray, to confess and repent, to search the Scriptures, or to seek justice for the socially cast off.

The church is by its very nature a community of formation. It is an ecology of spiritual guidance and care. It is the decisive context for lifelong training in Christianity. How we are formed depends so much upon who we are and what we do within this primary formative community.

Christian spiritual formation has to do with finding out through and with the help of the faith community

- how to be Christian in this time, in this place;
- how to recognize and confess our self-deception;
- how to walk according to the Spirit;
- how to recognize where we are refusing Christian Story and choosing instead the stories of culture and civil religion;
- how to acquire Christian character;
- how to learn the skills required by Christian Story, such as praying, meditating, repenting, loving, welcoming the stranger;
- how to actualize our Christian vocation over the course of a lifetime.

2

Drinking from Other Wells: A Partial Critique

This chapter explores the thesis that psychology is now the primary well from which contemporary Americans draw in their search for self-fulfillment. This is as true inside as outside the church. Within the American cultural ethos, the most powerful and pervasive contender with the Judeo-Christian tradition in furnishing metaphors decisive for Christian spirituality is the wellspring of modern psychology.

THE RISE OF PSYCHO-CULTURE

When we survey the terrain of psychological traditions influential in the contemporary American context, we can see five distinctive veins. They are traditional behaviorism (Skinner); classical psychoanalytic thought (Freud); humanistic, third force psychology (Maslow); transpersonal, fourth force psychology (Wilber); and structural-developmental theory (Piaget, Kohlberg). Taken together, these various psychologies form a basic fund of meanings and metaphors that we may refer to as "psycho-culture."[1]

Values proffered by psycho-culture make it difficult for believers to appropriate a distinctly Christian spirituality. This is *not* because modern psychology has nothing valuable to contribute to our self-understanding. Quite the contrary! It is because psychology has ceased properly to function as a science that simply investigates empirical data. Psychology has subtly taken over the role of moral and spiritual guidance. We can attribute this, in part, to the fact that the Protestant church allowed its own practice of spiritual direction to lapse.

In this respect, the most critical question to be posed to the church in the decade to come is this: Will our lives be oriented by the Judeo-Christian tradition, or will they increasingly gain their saliency from psycho-culture? From which well shall we drink? By what deep metaphors will our spirituality, our character, and our religious identity be nourished?[2]

The import of these questions may not readily be apparent. Commonly, we assume that psychology and theology ask and answer entirely different kinds of questions about human existence. Hence, there should be no conflict between the two disciples. We particularly think of humanistic and transpersonal psychology as being compatible with Christian claims, even as including implicit theological underpinnings. We have tended not to push beyond this assumption. We need, however, to uncover the deep metaphors of these psychologies and to bring them into critical dialogue with distinctly theological understandings of human becoming.

Don Browning and other philosophers of psychology have sufficiently pushed behind the superficial dissimilarities of theology and psychology to reveal how modern psychologies have ceased properly to be scientific. While they remain clothed in the aura of value-free science, they tend to commend an overall vision for human becoming.

Though they supposedly are sciences, modern technology and psychology alike have leaped out of their empirical scientific base to become inflated to mythic proportions. Humanistic and transpersonal psychologies have begun to function for us as quasi-religious "myths-of-becoming." That is, they operate as overall normative ways we see and orient ourselves within the world. As myths, they function as prescriptive interpretations of who we are to become as mature adults and *how* we are to negotiate that maturity. A myth, understood theologically, is not necessarily a falsehood. A myth is a metaphor for reality, construing how things ultimately are (a model *of*), and how we are to order our lives accordingly (a model *for*).

When the psychologies function for us as myths-of-becoming, they offer optimal images of human fulfillment, an implicit ethics, and a way to understand the ultimate context of our lives. Langdon Gilkey notes that this escalation has such an "under the table" quality that we are diverted from recognizing how scientific myths have broken into and replaced much of our religious tradition.

The inflation of psychology and technology to mythic proportions hinders rather than helps us to truthfully see ourselves. The more the psychologies remain specifically scientific tools, the more useful they are as such to Christian theology and Christian religious education. Psychology and theology equally need each other as well as other social science disciplines to illumine a holistic picture of human beings. Social science can supply this or that bit of data but cannot yield a picture of what it all ultimately means. Theology supplies that horizon.

Christian leaders share the common task of helping those whom they serve to fashion a coherent religious self-identity. Our basic character as human beings is constructed from disparate sources, not a single source. One of the most important skills in character formation is the ability to critically discern from which wells we drink. This means we must learn to sift and sort and to choose between the claims that compete for our loyalty.

Browning suggests that as we approach the psychologies looking for practical life guidance, we silently and tacitly ask ourselves basic questions about who we should be and what we should do with our lives.[3] I contend that in answering such questions, we are pervasively shaped by four distinctive (yet intertwining) trajectories within modern psycho-culture. These trajectories represent a triumph of psycho-cultural values over distinctly Christian theological claims to our spirituality. The four trajectories described in the following sections include the triumphs of (1) ethical egoism, (2) psychotherapy, (3) individualism, and (4) feminist ideology.

THE TRIUMPH OF ETHICAL EGOISM

Humanistic psychology orients its theory around notions of growth and change understood through the model of self-actualization. Self-actualization psychology at first blush seems quite congruent with such traditional theological themes as sanctification and transformation. What happens, however, when we push behind self-actualization theory to analyze its deeper vision of human becoming?

Vision of *Eudaimonia*: Know Thyself

According to David Norton's analysis, *eudaimonism* is the vision implicit within various humanistic self-actualization theories. The Greek notion of *eudaimonism* is that at birth every individual is perfectible according to her or his inner *daimon* or "true self." The great Greek imperative, "Know thyself," is often quoted in classic and contemporary spiritual literature. The self that one is to know is not the empirical self, the one that actually now exists. It is one's supposed "real" self, hidden deeply within. Through a great deal of effort, it is the ideal self that one may eventually become.

According to Norton, sculptors in pre-Hellenic Greece made busts of the semi-deity Silenus, each having a common trick. Hidden inside the hollow clay likeness was a golden figurine, revealed when the bust was opened. In Plato's *Symposium*, Alcibiades comments that Socrates is like a bust of Silenus. He is bald and potbellied on the outside, but those who perceive Socrates within the clay see one who is 'most divine.'

This episode is much more than a testimonial to Socrates by the drunken Alcibiades, says Norton. The testimonial makes use of the fundamental Greek conception of personhood. In the Greek understanding, not Socrates alone but every individual person is a bust of Silenus, inevitably flawed and misshapen in appearance to some degree but containing on the inside a golden figurine, one's good and true inner self *(daimon)*.[4]

Eudaimonism fuels many variations of the human potential movement and is expressed in the language of pop humanistic psychology. *Eudaimonism* essentially translates into a duty-to-self ethic. That is, its moral imperative is to discover and to develop one's inner self *(daimon)*. Browning refers to this stance as *ethical egoism*.[5] This does not mean that someone is necessarily selfish and rude. It means we take as a matter of principle that the human vocation is to maximize self-development.

In Norton's fully developed philosophy of *edaimonism*, we can detect that self-actualization is inflated into a quasi-religious perspective. Norton himself wishes to overcome the impersonalization and anomie of a modern technological society by helping each and every individual sense a unique destiny and calling. Yet does self-actualization theory adequately describe the human vocation? What does self-actualization theory suggest about the nature, dynamics, and tasks of spirituality?

The Move from Is to Ought

The self-actualization theorists commit a logical error called the *naturalistic fallacy*. That is, they translate what is noticed as a natural human tendency in many human beings into the ethical norm for all human beings. Whatever promotes inner self-development is the moral good; whatever blocks it is the bad.

When we shift the self-actualization impulse from the descriptive to the normative, it suddenly becomes a universal categorical imperative. Ethically, I *ought* to focus on my own inner desires, needs, and tendencies. I *ought* to depend on them as trustworthy guides in my life. I *ought* to learn to notice, name, and satisfy them. By always being true to my real, inner self, I have the surest guide to decision making over the course of my lifetime.

Self-actualization theory provides us with a vision of human becoming as well as with the guidelines by which to realize it. We become self-actualized by going after what philosophers call the nonmoral goods: mental health, self-knowledge, creativity, spontaneity, high self-esteem, the ability to share gut level feelings and to be true to felt needs. These become the key organizing images for spirituality and spiritual formation.

Based upon the primacy of the self, *eudaimonism* also confirms and inspires such basic American values as rugged individualism, self-help, and the right to personal happiness. The problem, of course, is that rather than setting these values in a larger (theological) frame of reference, spirituality is reduced to them. When spiritual disciplines pivot around these values, they are reduced, in the final analysis, to means for getting our own selves actualized.

THE TRIUMPH OF THE THERAPEUTIC

Philosophical ethical egoism seems to rule the day in the American cultural ethos, but its way was paved by "the triumph of the therapeutic." This trajectory has been documented by Philip Rieff in his book of the same title.[6]

Rieff argues that, traditionally, intimate communities bonded by trust and care functioned to sustain persons in emotional and spiritual health. This is no longer the case. Instead, the therapeutic motif, translated from the psychoanalytic tradition to other modern psychologies, promotes therapeutic networks that now replace more traditional forms of community.

In Robert Bellah's perspective, the therapeutic aspects of American culture underwrite the ethic of self-actualization.[7] Because its implicit values are autonomy, independence and self-sufficiency, the private therapy motif reinforces in American culture an already eroded sense of community and interdependency. The therapeutic motif, furthermore, tempts us to think about spirituality as simply another means to mental health.

Within the therapeutic model, spiritual discipline is "successful" when the individual has achieved an inner sense of warmth and well-being. Certainly, God is the Eternal One who brings peace to a divided heart, but God is also the convictor, the confronter, the challenger.[8] Rarely we do see this side of God in the therapeutic model. For all that this brand of spirituality is worth, quips Urban Holmes, one might as well substitute a warm bath!

The self-therapy motif is also fed from the streams of transpersonalism. As transpersonal psychology informs contemporary spirituality, the assumptions are that (1) the altered or higher states of human consciousness afford the normative means of participating in divine reality and that (2) the host of techniques culled from Eastern mystical psychologies enable individuals to achieve such altered states.

Expansion of consciousness is no guarantee of expanding human freedom and responsibility. Besides, ecstatic states throughout human history more often have been the by-products or accompaniments of religious insight and creativity and subsequent repentance. Of more interest than altered states of consciousness per se are those transforming moments when our hearts are altered. These are times when we find ourselves freed to love instead of to fear, to forgive instead of to retaliate, to hope instead of to despair.

The therapeutic motif has triumphed not only in the wider American culture but also in the pastoral and diaconal offices of the church. Many pastors and educators are shaped in their work more by psychological disciplines than by a distinctly Christian theology. The most common guiding image for pastors, priests, and educators is a composite of the corporate manager and the psychotherapist. The therapist, equally like the corporate manager, says Bellah, is a "specialist in mobilizing resources for effective action, only here the resources are largely internal to the individual and the measure of effectiveness is the elusive critierion of personal satisfaction."[9]

Pastors and educators today tend to know more about analyzing the human psyche than they do about caring for the human soul. Yet as Ruth Barnhouse notes, guidance of human souls is in fact the oldest profession! Every culture and time has had its shamans, confessors, gurus, spiritual directors, wise men and women. Only in the last century have we bifurcated the ancient profession into a religious and a secular branch.[10] Since the church unfortunately allowed its own ministry of spiritual direction to lapse, Christian believers and leaders alike have turned to the secular model as the most readily available source of soul care.

Within the secular branch, though, guidance is aimed at the psyche, not the soul. In psychotherapy, moreover, *seelsorge* ("soul care") is not the gift or function of a community of many ordinary saints. Care is purchased (whether there is a fee or not) through contractual arrangements with individual therapists or support groups. This maintains a formality and a distance that is protective of privacy. The therapeutic model creates consumers who purchase community—not to mention spiritual guidance!—in the marketplace. Yet the care generated therein is not permanent. When the fee is paid, the obligation to care for each other is over.

THE TRIUMPH OF INDIVIDUALISM

The strands of psycho-culture all tend to converge in leading individuals to think of their various obligations, including those of marriage, work, religion, and politics, as means to individual fulfillment rather than as moral imperatives and spiritual commitments.[11] The language of psycho-culture emphasizes almost exclusively the inner needs, wishes, and desires of the individual *qua* individual, not as an active and committed member of a community of care. Values implicit in psycho-culture produce people who operate largely out of psychic drives and needs. The net effect is the isolation of persons from public concerns. In fact, one's motto becomes "I participate only to the extent that it gets me self-developed."

In the hands of psycho-culture, spirituality slips into a solitary and private affair. Implicitly we are left with a rather narrow vision of the human self as autonomous, atomistic, and self-contained. Jean Elshtain notes that the model of self in humanistic psychology seeks only private virtue, retreating from the world under the guise of openness to it. For the self-actualizing self, "any old social locus is fine, for freedom lies within, in a 'feeling' rather than within complicated personal-political ties and social arrangements."[12] Within self-development philosophy, there are no moral and spiritual imperatives, only optional strategies for self-fulfillment!

Bellah's recent work in *Habits of the Heart* calls attention to the individualism run amok in contemporary culture, infecting every dimension and value of life. He documents how our "American cultural traditions define personality, achievement, and the purpose of human life in ways that leave the individual suspended in glorious, but terrifying, isolation."[13]

Bellah outlines the modes of individualism that have dominated American culture from its earliest colonization to the present. Basic to individualism overall is the old philosophical strand in American culture that sees social life as an arrangement for the fulfillment of the needs of individuals. Individualism is the very taproot of American culture and religion. A Lockean, almost ontological individualism holds sway, notes Bellah, in virtually every dimension of culture, especially in religion. In the Lockean tradition, the individual is prior to society, the self being the main form or fundamental unit of reality. Society is formed only through voluntary contracts for the self-interested good of individuals. Most Americans, in fact, see the church in this light, approaching it from an extremely voluntaristic stance.

The fact that the sphere of individualism is being widened by modern psychologies and psychotherapies shrinks the likelihood that spirituality will become any less individualistic *unless* American churches are able to show how participation in a faith community and a religious tradition is able to sustain, rather than erode, authentic individuality.

THE TRIUMPH OF FEMINIST IDEOLOGY

For many writers, especially feminists, recovery of spirituality means recovery of the feminine side of Christianity into the church. This means not only welcoming the gifts of women's leadership in the church but also recovering what is called the feminine pole or principle within humanity as a whole, and within each individual human being.

In this trend, many contemporary writers in spirituality appeal to the depth psychology of Carl Jung. He believed that the human psyche is comprised of both a feminine (anima) and a masculine (animus) dimension. No individual is whole who does not develop the feminine-masculine polarity within her- or himself. Feminine and masculine in this sense do not strictly have to do with our sexuality or genitality, but with certain modalities of relating to the world and of internalizing reality.

Though I am, of course, happy about the emerging appreciation of the feminine mode, I do not agree with those writers who identify Christian spirituality *exclusively* with the so-called feminine side of the human psyche. While both the spiritual and the feminine have been lost in the church, their simultaneous recovery is no simple equation. To equate strictly the spiritual with the feminine does not do justice to either one. I am concerned that some writers lapse into a romanticizing, ideologizing, and therefore trivializing of the feminine.

Some of the current uses made of Jungian psychology, in fact, create a new eclipse. For instance, some literature leaves the unfortunate impression that spirituality refers to the feminine pole while not including the masculine, to feeling that excludes thinking, to intuition and not cognition, to the transrational and not the rational, to whatever is associated with the right rather than the left brain.

Not only is the spiritual associated only with the feminine, but it is also implied that modes associated with the masculine are corrupt, evil, and distorted, or at least that they have no truck with the spiritual. Everything associated with the feminine principle is viewed as harmonious, good, whole, and uncorrupted.

What a reversal! The old dualism is converted to a new dualism that assigns goodness to feminine modalities and evil to masculine modalities. It asserts that feminine modes, if not women themselves, are more naturally holistic, self-integrated, and spiritual. The plain truth is that imagination, intuition, and feeling can become as distorted as reason and intellect. The obvious mistake here is the sacralization of the feminine pole over against the masculine, replacing one eclipse with another and reversing rather than overcoming the dualism. We tend to forget that both the feminine and the masculine require a normative horizon within which to gain their saliency.

In the final analysis, this trend serves *not* to liberate women but in fact to ideologize the very things feminists seek to overcome. Oddly enough, romanticizing the feminine does not move us further toward dismantling patriarchy. This is precisely because it so strongly downplays those qualities, associated with the masculine, that are needed to unmask patriarchy: intellect, reason, critical inquiry, and confrontation. Such downplaying, furthermore, does no more than to play into the hands of the anti-intellectual bias of American culture.

When valorized as only the feminine side of Christianity, the full richness of "walking in the Spirit" is maimed and crippled. Unfortunately, the Holy Spirit throughout Christian tradition has tended to be associated with passivity, subordination, dependency, the inner life, and the psychology of feelings. Yet these tendencies strip the Spirit of its social effects and its political, prophetic role in the church. In her book *Metaphors for the Contemporary Church*, Susan Thistlethwaite demonstrates how the history of thought about the Holy Spirit has alternated between keeping it tied to the visible, institutional church, on the one hand, and relegating it to the believer's interior life, on the other. In either case, we both undervalue and circumscribe the action of the Spirit. We are robbed of appreciation for the public, prophetic acts of the Spirit and for the Spirit's role in sustaining human interdependencies.[14] Yet in the Scriptures we see a Spirit who empowers us to discern, to confront, and to resist the dehumanizing "powers and principalities" of any age.

A liberating (and thus by definition a truly feminist) spirituality *balances* and *integrates* the cognitive and the affective, the rational and the transrational, the mind and the body, the passive and the active, the conscious and the unconscious, the capacity to receive and the capacity to resist. A liberating and liberated spirituality realizes that both men and women are fallen from Eden. Just as it unmasks the gods of male superiority, it also denies the ideology of female moral and spiritual superiority.

Holistic spirituality, furthermore, does not categorically assign such qualities as mutuality, nurture, and care to the so-called "feminine," but recognizes them as fundamental *human* qualities revealed decisively in the person of Jesus and empowered in us by our participation in the Story he lived among us.

SUMMARY

Psycho-culture would have us believe that the key to our spiritual existence lies deeply hidden within the individual unconscious or else within the collective unconscious. The Christian Gospel tells us, to the contrary, that something decisive has been given to us *extra nos,* from outside ourselves. Access to that divinely given reality is provided to us through the symbolic language of the believing community.

Cultivating Christian spirituality requires learning a particular language. To learn any new language requires learning a new vocabulary, as well as the rules for its use. Spiritual guidance, therefore, is less a matter of drawing out than of *bringing to.* We do not draw language out of people! We make it accessible to them. We teach them how to use it.

3

Participation: Theological Foundations

Spirituality, as I have defined it, is our self-transcendent capacity to recognize and to respond to God's creative and redemptive activity in all of creation. This chapter explores theological symbols and themes that pattern our participation in God's redemptive work in the world, symbolized as the Realm of God. It is the task of Christian education and spiritual guidance to initiate believers, through the faith community, into the coming of God's Realm and to help them understand and live their whole lives in light of that reality.

PARTICIPATING IN THE REALM OF GOD

Theology in recent decades has been shifting its focus from the Christ above to the Jesus below. With this shift, more attention is being given to what Jesus preached and taught, accompanied by a growing consensus that the church should preach and teach what Jesus did: the Realm of God. Jesus came preaching "The time is fulfilled, and the kingdom of God is at hand; repent, and believe in the gospel" (Mark 1:15). Not only did Jesus announce that he was sent to preach

God's Realm (Luke 4:43), but he also commissioned his followers to do the same (cf. Matt. 10:7; Luke 10:8-9).

As a symbol that points to human history as the arena of God's redemptive actions, the meaning of the Realm of God can never be exhausted. The term does not refer to a place but to a dynamic Way of life. Realm of God refers to God's presence and activity in human affairs. We are called to participate with a God who mends our broken existence and knits us into a community that actively searches out the stranger.

Theologically speaking, talk about the Realm of God is gathered up under the theological rubric of *eschatology*, now seen as a central theme from which other theological themes derive their meaning. Eschatology has to do with the final, definitive meaning of life. It refers to God's ultimate and final intentions for humanity and for all of creation. Jesus himself belonged to the prophetic eschatological tradition. A study of key eschatological passages in the Old and New Testaments yields dynamic pictures of the Realm of God in human history.[1] Our *gift*, our *promise*, and our *challenge* is to participate now, *as the church*, in the Way of life as disclosed in these images. They reveal to us our promised destiny as children of God, as daughters and sons of Sarah and Abraham, as co-heirs with Christ.

1. *The Realm of God is a shocking and radical reversal of the usual order of things.* Through biblical images we see the New Creation pictured as (1) a dynamic interaction (2) between different people and between elements of creation (3) of a different, surprising sort, (4) which turns the world's usual experience and expectations upside down!

The parables, for instance, are always stories about people who relate in fundamentally new and surprising ways. Relationships on every level are reordered. There is an alternative shaping of human life, countervailing the dominant culture. Neighbors and nations dwell in peace.

Everyone's well-being is considered. The hungry are fed; orphans, widows, the poor, and the naked are cared for, the strangers are welcomed. There is no one without the minimum necessities of life. There is justice for the oppressed, and hospitality for the dispossessed.

Enemies and strangers sit down and feast together at the same banquet table; they are gathered from north, south, east, and west. The atmosphere is marked by festive celebration and thanksgiving. Eucharistic hospitality is based on this reality, as we offer to the world an open table, an open heart, an open community!

People are active! There's no lolling around on white clouds here. People build, inhabit, plant, harvest, share, eat, rejoice. Everyone enjoys the fruit of his or her own labor: "They shall not build and another inhabit" (Isa. 65:22). The impossible and unlikely happens! There is hope where there was no hope! To enter into God's Realm is to enter the fullness of life that God intends.

In this light, we are called to actively oppose all social and interpersonal arrangements that do not reflect the values of the New Age. God's Realm is a vision of reality that is to be concretely expressed in the way we shape our life together.

2. *Jesus Christ is the decisive revelation of God's Realm in human history.* Jesus never defined God's Realm for us. Rather, he told stories of it, mainly through the parables. Not only did he tell the stories, Jesus *was* that Realm. Origen called Christ the *autobasileia.* To experience Jesus Christ is to experience the New Humanity. God's Realm *has* come decisively, in Jesus' life, death, and resurrection, *is* coming into history, and *will come* in final glory.

Many church hymns are about the kingdom of God (or kingdom of Heaven—there is no difference). Sometimes the songs image Heaven as a "promised land," but more accurately, Heaven symbolizes a promised *condition* of life (Dorothy Söelle). This condition or Way of life has burst in upon us in the coming of Jesus! "Being asked by the Pharisees when the Kingdom of God was coming, he answered them, 'The Kingdom of God is not coming with signs to be observed; nor will they say, "Lo, here it is!" or "There!" for behold, the Kingdom of God is in the midst of you!'" (Luke 17:21).

Participation in the coming of God's Realm is therefore Christ-centered. We are baptized "into Christ" (Gal. 3:27). Although it is through creation that God bestows on us our gift of participation, Christ the Second Adam redefines the context of our participation from creation to the New Age. In him we see what it means to become citizens of the Realm of God. Christ bears the image of the New Humanity into which we are being conformed.[2] God breaks through the borders of our definitions of what it means to be a human being to give a new and startling picture of the human in Jesus!

Jesus Christ teaches us how to live for others (Phil. 2:4-5). To live the Story that Jesus lived (Phil. 2:6-8), to live for others, is to be led to the unwanted, the unemployed, the uncared for, the hungry and homeless (Matt. 25). "In the garden alone" is not the best place to find Christ! Christ came into the world to put our spirituality in its proper perspective, says Mother Teresa.[3]

> God has identified himself with the hungry, the sick, the naked, the homeless; hunger not only for bread, but for love, for care, to be somebody to someone; nakedness, not of clothing only, but nakedness of that compassion that very few people give to the unknown; homelessness, not only just for a shelter made of stone, but that homelessness that comes from having no one to call your own.[4]

3. *God's Realm is received and not generated by human effort.* It is a gift. We receive the gift by doing *this* rather than *that* as a response to God's active rule. The invitation is not to usher in the Realm. It is to participate in a New Age that comes only

"by the finger of God" (Luke 11:20). Since it is a gift, we are freed to celebrate it in freedom, joy, and peace. Those present include both the sinners and the sinned against. Out of the utter freedom of God, both receive because both need the gifts of God's mercy and grace.

Because it is a gift, the growth of God's Realm in the world is beyond human understanding or human control. Yet persons may recognize its progress and participate in its coming (Mark 4:10ff.; Luke 8). Though persons may *suppose* that they highly prize it, they may in fact be rejecting invitations in their midst to enter and participate (Luke 14:15-24).

4. *The invitation to God's Realm is an invitation to embrace a covenantal way of life.* This is because salvation is inclusive and communally oriented. The focus is on "we," "our," and "us." The inbreaking of God's Realm opens up community, creates community, reconciles community. We participate in its coming when we show unbounded concern for the well-being of the neighbor and radical hospitality to the stranger. Neighbors are revealed to include persons *unlike* us (Luke 10:29-37). According to Jesus, when we prove ourselves neighbors in a radical fashion, we "are not far from the kingdom of God" (Mark 12:34).

A covenantal way of life means more than the coziness of like-minded people. Jesus revealed covenant to mean *actively* searching out persons who seem not to fit the status quo. A covenant community is not particularly a homogeneous enclave. It is to include "the poor, the maimed, the lame, the blind," the illiterate, the aged, the retarded (Luke 14:12-14).

The fact of covenant teaches us to see all those whom God creates and loves as our brothers and sisters in Christ. All other human criteria of association, therefore, are relativized! Church growth movements that seek to build community on principles of homogeneity or anything other than the new covenant in Christ promote a pseudobasis for community and eventually yield bogus intimacy, bogus spirituality, and bogus discipleship.

5. *The community of faith, the church, is called to be the sign and sacrament of the world God wills.* The church is where we come within sight of God's Realm and where we are initiated into it. But God's redemptive activity is not confined to the church. An important biblical image referring to God's activity and rule is *oikia* (household; see Mark 3:24-25), originally referring to God's redemptive work in the whole created order. As Letty Russell points out, in later New Testament traditions, *oikia* or *oikos* (household) as a New Creation metaphor dissolves gradually into a church-centered metaphor.[5] Rather than serving as an image of God's Realm in all creation, the household became an image for the church. Yet these two references must exist in dynamic tension.

The household obviously is not a place but a network of activity and relationships. Whether referring to the church or to God's Realm, the invitation is the same: to be built into God's creative and redemptive activity in the world, for the sake of the world. As a sign and sacrament, the church exists to embody, to display and to mediate God's grace in the world.

The church's *first* task, therefore, is not to go out and change the world, claims Stanley Hauerwas. The church must first of all become itself, plainly enough for the world to see that there exists for it a New Creation. The faithfulness of the church's service depends upon its ability to convincingly point to the presence of God in human history. Thus, as Hauerwas notes, our type of service may appear ineffective in the eyes of the world. The service the church is called to provide is to demonstrate that Jesus made possible a new social order and a new world.[6] The church is to reflect the shape of redeemed existence.

6. *Participation in the coming of God's Realm requires our*

complete and ongoing reorientation, a permanent metanoia or conversion. Throughout a lifetime we must turn and return to God's redemptive presence. Conversion, understood biblically, is demanded as much from believers as nonbelievers! In order to fully participate, we must die time and again to intolerance, vengeance, despair, and self-preoccupation and be born again to compassion, hospitality, mutuality, love, and forgiveness.

The new birth we receive in baptism is an ongoing metanoia, a lifelong reorientation to God in Christ. As members of a fallen people, we continually fall back into sin and alienation. The Spirit, given in our baptism, frees us again and again to "put on" our new nature: "Put off your old nature which belongs to your former manner of life and is corrupt . . . and be renewed in the spirit of your minds, and put on the new nature, created after the likeness of God" (Eph. 4:22-24).

The baptismal clothing metaphor (to "put on" and "put off") was effective for the writer of Ephesians to use with early hearers, for to them garments signified the real person. A person was incorporated into a new community, another age group, office, or status, by throwing off the old clothing and being vested with a white baptismal shirt, a marriage gown, monastic garb, a priest's stole, or another garment. Changes of clothing meant a real change in the person. We are given our new identity in baptism, yet we grow into our baptismal garments throughout the rest of our lives. We never outgrow them.

7. *Participation in the coming of God's Realm requires freedom and creates freedom.* "Now the Lord is the Spirit, and where the Spirit of the Lord is, there is freedom" (II Cor. 3:17). Participation requires inner and outer freedom from all that binds us. Jesus did not say that the truth would make us spiritual; rather, the truth shall set us free (John 8:31, 36). In

the New Testament witness, Jesus explicitly re-presents God's gift of freedom in his own coming:

> The Spirit of the Lord is upon me,
> because he has anointed me to preach good news to the poor.
> He has sent me to proclaim release to the captives
> and recovering of sight to the blind,
> to set at liberty those who are oppressed,
> to proclaim the acceptable year of the Lord. (Luke 4:18-19)

To the apostle Paul's mind we are created for "glorious freedom" as children of God (Rom. 8:21). According to the biblical story, to be created in the image and likeness of God means to be created in the image of a free, creative, and whole person. Our longing for freedom, along with the real possibility of actualizing it, owes to the gift of *imago Dei* to each and every one of us.

As finite human beings, though, we continually run away from the freedom and wholeness for which we were created. The biblical story uses the metaphors of fallenness, brokenness, and bondage in order to talk about our actual condition, which is a state of *un*-freedom.

To be a Christian means to look to Jesus, who redefines for us what freedom means. Through him we receive our freedom: "For freedom Christ has set us free" (Gal. 5:1). Jesus Christ is the one who summons us to live in freedom as God's children and the one through whom that freedom is now possible. Faith and trust in God's love, made explicit in Jesus Christ, grounds us in the freedom *from* and *for* ourselves, and *from* and *for* all things.[7]

8. *Since we live "between the times," our participation in the Realm of God is provisional.* Because we are finite, our participation in God's Realm is broken, incomplete, and provisional. We live in the "already but not yet" reality of God's Realm: "Now in putting everything in subjection to him, he left nothing outside his control. [But] as it is, we do

not yet see everything in subjection to him. But we see Jesus" (Heb. 2:8*b*-9*a*). Alongside our experience of the New Age are also signs and experience of risk, defeat, and the cross.[8]

Because it is between the times, our participation is measured by faithfulness, not effectiveness as determined by cultural standards (usually numerically measured!). The Christian life is not at all based upon success but rather upon a foretaste of the New Creation, defined not by perfection but by parabolic power.[9] All that God requires of us is our faithfulness; it is up to society to decide how to respond.

9. *By the power of the Holy Spirit we participate in the coming of God's Realm.* The experience of Spirit is primal in our experience as Christians, for "it is the Spirit himself bearing witness with our spirit that we are children of God" (Rom. 8:16). In biblical terms, to live and walk by the Spirit (Gal. 5:25) is to participate in the power of God's New Age (I Cor. 4:20).

Since the Spirit is the earnest or the down payment of the New Age, to live by the Spirit is to live in the freedom of our promised future in Jesus Christ. In the Spirit, we anticipate the future, we are empowered for the future, we receive our future. The Spirit animates our hope in this future and seals us into our inheritance: "In him you also, who have heard the word of truth, the gospel of your salvation, and have believed in him, were sealed with the promised Holy Spirit, which is the guarantee of our inheritance until we acquire possession of it, to the praise of his glory" (Eph. 1:13-14).

10. *The Realm of God embraces the fullness of the human condition, as well as of all creation.* God's Realm is more than a message of personal consolation, more than fire insurance for future salvation, more than a private, inner religious experience. God's Realm embraces *all* dimensions of human existence, beginning here and now. God is present in all corners of creation, acting to overcome the forces of death and destruction.

God works not only to set the prisoner free but also to transform conditions that imprison, whether they are interpersonal, social, or economic. We see this, for instance, in the eschatological images of Isaiah 65:17-23:

> For behold, I create new heavens and a new earth;
> ....
> . . . I create Jerusalem a rejoicing,
> and her people a joy. . . .
>
> ....
> no more shall be heard in it the sound of weeping
> and the cry of distress.
> No more shall there be in it
> an infant that lives but a few days,
> or an old man who does not fill out his days,
> for the child shall die a hundred years old,
> and the sinner a hundred years old shall be accursed.
> They shall build houses and inhabit them;
> they shall plant vineyards and eat their fruit.
> They shall not build and another inhabit;
> they shall not plant and another eat;
>
> ....
> They shall not labor in vain,
> or bear children for calamity.

Imagine a city where there is no racial strife and where minimum human needs are more than met! Where wage earners are not exploited by the rich! Where there are no homeless! Where there are no poor, hungry people! The Scriptures invite us to imagine this as the kind of city into which God is building us.

God's eschatological Realm, as we can see, is a vision out of which we must make concrete, bold decisions. The Scriptures give us vivid images of how human relationships on all levels are to be ordered in God's Realm. The vision compels us, if we truly are to participate in God's work, to pose a critique of all social constructions of power and authority that do not recognize God as Creator and as Redeemer of history.

11. *The spiritual disciplines, especially the sacraments, make visible God's Realm in the world.* As eschatological in nature, the sacraments point us to "the already but not yetness" of God's Realm. They play a role in making visible to Christians both justice and injustice.[10] The foretaste of God's Realm that we receive in the Eucharist, for example, creates in us a yearning for its fullness and sensitizes us to the pain of its not-yetness. We do in fact prepare and feast at the Table in the presence of all kinds of enemies.[11] We display sumptuous eating, while many go hungry. Although our gathering at the Table gives us a foretaste of the Great Banquet, the images that we share compel us to ask why things are not *now* like this. The Eucharist calls into question our present social arrangements and is at the same time a source of power for their change and transformation.

If we truly believe the message they mediate, the sacraments will break us away from cultural norms. Unless coopted by culture, they are radical-countercultural ways of living, drawing us more fully into God's redemptive work.

12. *Baptism is our ordination into the ministry of God's Realm in the world.* Baptism is one of the chief means, as James White points out, through which we Christians receive God's self-giving.[12] Through baptism all Christians are ordained into the gift of participating in all that God is and does for us.

The early Christians used images drawn from ordinary daily life, rather than explicitly theological language, to talk about their experience of baptism, images such as birth, washing, putting on clothes, death and burial.[13]

According to White, there are five images central to an early Christian or New Testament view of baptism:[14] (1) Through baptism we are united to Jesus Christ and his work, and given a share in the ministry of reconciliation and redemption (II Cor. 5:18). (2) Through baptism we are incorporated into Christ's body on earth, the church (I Cor. 12:13). (3) Through baptism we are given the Holy Spirit as a foretaste of our full inheritance and full participation as daughters and sons in the Realm of God (Eph. 1:13-14). (4) Through baptism our sins are forgiven, we are cleansed, and the image of God within is restored (Acts 22:16). (5) Through baptism we are reborn, from the womb of God, of water and the Spirit, completely dependent on God's tenderness, mercy, and love (II Cor. 5:17).

Like our biological birth, we do not control the conditions of our rebirth through baptism. Through the waters God recreates us into something we were not. God makes us Christians, giving us a share in the mending of creation, and the knitting up of human community.

SUMMARY

In summary, the Christian spiritual life is nothing less than our free participation as self-agents in God's creative and redemptive activity in all of creation *(oikoumene)*. Spiritual discipline includes those practices and actions indispensible to actualizing our freedom to participate. Through catching us up into its Story, the faith community trains us to see where and how God is at work mending creation, and how we, too, may participate.

This model of spirituality stands over against a minimalist understanding, that is, spirituality as a litany of (introspective) practices designed to meet the dictum "know thyself" or "actualize thyself." Spiritual disciplines gain their saliency because of the part they play in a whole way of life. Too many modern men and women want to "technicize" the spiritual life. The temptation is to dissect it from the faith community and to turn it into a program. Christian spirituality is, however, a complex and costly living of the Story that Christ lived among us (Phil. 2:6 NEB).

4

Participation: Practical Foundations

In this chapter, we shall explore various human actions that express, shape and discipline our lives as Christians. As with the church in every age, we each must decide and redecide to participate in the coming of God's Realm. Something must actually happen through our own self-involvement and active contribution. There is a grammar and a logic to our participation in God's triune reality, supplied by those practices we call the spiritual disciplines.

We are formed as Christians by engaging *with the church* in certain tangible, communal, personal, and difficult practices. They are the actual things we do attitudinally, bodily, and repeatedly, as basic to becoming Christian. To engage in those practices together *is* to engage in spiritual discipline, *is* to participate in God's Realm, *is* to become Christian, and *is* to be the church together.

This carries our understanding of spiritual disciplines beyond a litany of techniques used to focus on the interior life or on self-actualization. Spiritual disciplines are ways to get us out of ourselves, not into ourselves! Through their practice we are drawn out of self-absorption and into following Christ (Matt. 25).

There is no normative number or checklist of disciplines; they can be mapped out in various ways. Whatever else may be said, there are at least seven affirmations fundamental to understanding and undertaking a disciplined spiritual life.

1. *Through the spiritual disciplines we remember, anticipate, and participate in God's story of creation and redemption.* A central claim of this book is that Christian spirituality is rooted in the call to anticipate and to participate in the coming of God's Realm. Spiritual disciplines are specific, concrete, bodily means by which we remember our part in God's Story and anticipate the fullness of God's Realm in Jesus Christ. The disciplines are the basic means by which the church initiates us into the coming of God's Realm.

Through the disciplines, we remember the sweep of God's creating and reconciling work in the world. The Greek word *anamnesis* means "a calling to mind" or "a remembrance," yet so much more is implied. To remember is to experience *anew*. The biblical insight is that we are instructed and shaped by what we remember. Our remembered past and our anticipated future associate with each other decisively in our present. The key, therefore, is for us to form a redemptive memory and a hopeful imagination.

2. *Through the spiritual disciplines we posture ourselves to receive and to actualize God's grace in our lives,* anticipating the day when all things are made new (Rev. 21:5). There are particular ways that we appropriate God's grace into our daily lives. The church traditionally called these practices "the *means of grace.*" John Wesley also described them as "works of piety" and "works of mercy." Churches today are speaking of them as the spiritual disciplines.

John Wesley considered the means of grace to be the heart of Christian spiritual discipline. In his sermon entitled "The Means of Grace," Wesley described them as outward signs, words, and actions appointed by God to be the channels through which God *ordinarily* conveys grace to us. The extraordinary claim is that God acts in and through quite ordinary, visible, and sensual means for us and our salvation. Wesley insisted that the means by which we experience and appropriate grace are varied and many and can be combined together in a thousand different ways.[1] Grace is not trapped into God's own instituted means!

Wesley, therefore, distinguished between *instituted* and *provisional* means of grace. For him, the *instituted* means of grace include the sacraments of Eucharist and baptism, prayer and meditation, searching the Scriptures, and confession and repentance. These means were instituted by God for the church's sake. In its emphasis on *sola scriptura* the Protestant church unfortunately wound up neglecting the sacraments, whereas the Roman Catholic church neglected the Bible as a means of appropriating grace.

In his own ministry, Wesley relied heavily on the provisional means of grace, which included his well-known bands, class meetings, and Christian conferences. Provisional means of grace are non-normative; that is, as techniques they are experimental and are exchangeable for more helpful strategies. Examples popular today are journal keeping and dream recording, alongside traditional *lectio divina* and the Jesus Prayer.

3. *Through the spiritual disciplines we not only receive grace, but we also mediate signs of grace to and in the world.* Gabriel Fackre calls the spiritual disciplines the "sign language" of Christian faith.[2] They make visible to the world God's self-giving and God's intention to create a New Humanity. As such, spiritual disciplines are gestures of the church that *do* what they *say;* they convey grace as well as display grace.[3] When we give a cup of cold water, for example, it is much more than a private matter. The act is an event in the redemption of the human community, an instance of our

participation in the world God wills.[4] If we truly believe the message they mediate, the means of grace will break us away from cultural norms.[5]

For Wesley, "works of mercy" are means of grace that have particular impact as sign language to the world. Viewed as ways we respond to the full range of human need, whether the need relates to souls or bodies,[6] works of mercy include actions such as

> feeding the hungry, clothing the naked, entertaining the stranger, visiting those that are in prison, or sick, or variously afflicted, such as the endeavoring to instruct the ignorant, to awaken the stupid sinner, to quicken the lukewarm, to confirm the wavering, to comfort the feeble-minded, to succour the tempted, or contribute in any manner to the saving of souls from death.[7]

These actions, therefore, are not to be regarded as "social outreach" counterposed to spirituality; they are means of grace vital to our spiritual discipline and our formation as Christians.

4. *Through the spiritual disciplines we express our Christian self-identity.* Christian spirituality begins with an inward bias that is then expressed in outward actions. In this sense, patriotism provides a good analogy. Patriotism is a basic posture of life, expressed by certain gestures like singing the national anthem and saluting the American flag. These are public and communal, not private, practices. We do these things because we *already* are patriotic, not because we wish to become so.

Spiritual discipline follows this analogy. We engage in particular practices because of who we are already through God's grace. We are a pentecostal people. We live by the invocation of the Spirit. As the *koinonia*, we are people adopted into a household, bound together and sealed into a promised future by the Spirit. The spiritual disciplines are bold expressions of this self-identity.

5. *Concomitantly, through the spiritual disciplines our Christian self-identity is decisively shaped and formed.* Disciplines not only express who we are, however. They also help form us into what we were not. Through their sustained practice, we become Christian and mature in Christian character. Disciplines posture our bodies and our souls so that we may be formed to be as the Christian Story is. Through them we become living reminders of Jesus Christ in the world.

Following the analogy of patriotism, from childhood onward we engage in certain exercises together so that they will inspire and create patriotism in us. Likewise, as the church engages us together in the means of grace, a deeper sense of Christian self-identity is inspired and formed in us. Whatever else we consider the spiritual disciplines to be, they are the basic rudiments by which we become Christian.

The formative power of the spiritual disciplines, particularly the sacraments, derives in large measure from their nature as nonverbal sign language. The sacraments essentially are symbolic actions to which words are linked. Sacramental actions touch us far more deeply than can words alone. They exert their greatest influence on us at prereflective and preconscious levels. In fact, claims James White, the experience of the weekly gestures joined with familiar words has a far deeper power to form us than any single sermon could ever have.[8]

6. *Through the disciplined spiritual life we acquire deep and abiding dispositions, or habits of the heart.* Christian virtues or habits of the heart tend to be overlooked as essential spiritual disciplines. Jonathan Edwards called them religious affections, meaning much more than fleeting feelings. Religious affections are deep and abiding dispositions or motives that become our own as we practice the "mind" of Christ (Phil. 2:5). Edwards believed, in fact, that the Christian faith *is* a pattern of deep affections.

The word "discipline" refers to the training required to

develop a particular kind of character. In Latin a *discipulus* is a learner. Christian spiritual discipline is a matter of forming our character around the affections, attitudes, and actions fitting to the Christian story.

Religious affections have recently been explored by Don Saliers in *The Soul in Paraphrase: Prayer and the Religious Affections.* Similar to Edwards, Saliers views affections as religious teachings assimilated by the heart. As such, they are not simply heat without light. Basic affections include gratitude and giving thanks, holy fear and repentance, joy and suffering, and love of God and neighbor. Since religious affections are fundamental aspects of our character, we are held accountable for the dispositions that dwell in the center of our hearts.

7. *Through the spiritual disciplines we remember our baptism, realize our vocation, and fulfill our Christian calling in the world.* "I . . . beg you to lead a life worthy of the calling to which you have been called. . . . There is one body and one Spirit, just as you were called to the one hope that belongs to your call, one Lord, one faith, one baptism, one God" (Eph. 4:1, 4-6*a*). The aim of spiritual discipline is not self-actualization, but rather realization of our baptism throughout a lifetime. Through baptism we are adopted into a covenant community and introduced to our fundamental human vocation. The word "vocation" is from the Latin *vocatio,* meaning "summons," and the past principle *vocare,* "to call." Biblical faith construes human vocation *(klesis)* in terms of our call to participate in all that God is and does.

Baptism, seen in this light, means that our self-identity is a gift; it is not self-derived. Once we had no identity; now we do! The baptismal life frees us to become the unique person each of us really is. This is both our gift and our call. Says Rabbi Susya, "In the world to come I shall not be asked: 'Why were you not Moses?' I shall be asked: 'Why were you not Susya?' "[9]

> After the fire a still small voice. And when Elijah heard it, he wrapped his face in his mantle and went out. . . . And behold, there came a voice to him, and said, "What are you doing here, Elijah?" (I Kings 19:11-13)

"What are you doing here, Susanne?" "What are you doing here, John?" This question is one that God puts not only to Elijah. God addresses this question to every one of us. It is the question by which we are to orient our entire lives. What are you doing here? What are you doing with your life in this place, at this moment?

How do you remember your baptism? What kind of person are you becoming? Do you wish to become? What are you sowing with your life? What gifts do you have for the good of the faith community? For the global human community?

Who has loved you, cared for you, and invested in you? In whom do you invest and for whom and what do you care? What is it that orients your life? What gives you joy, hope, and purpose?

These questions, posed by our baptism, are vocational questions rather than questions of self-actualization. For the Christian, the biblical metaphor of covenant transposes all questions of self-actualization into vocational questions.[10] Our God is One who wills, who makes, and who keeps covenant with us. Covenant is a deep and pervasive affirmation, writes Walter Brueggemann, that we utterly depend upon the One who initiates and who wills far more good for us than we do for ourselves.[11]

Vocation, thus, is not our profession, not our career, not our job, and not our volunteer or church work. Our vocation, in terms of covenant faith, is to participate in the most fully conscious way we can in the triune life of God, whatever our job or profession may be. Vocation includes the response we make with our total selves to God's self-giving, which we come to know in and through the church.

Any intentional approach to spiritual formation, therefore,

must begin with attention to vocation and proceed by asking vocational questions. We begin with an exploration and assessment of our own unique starting place *(archai)*. From that standpoint, with the help of companions we discern the inner direction of our deepest desires, our gifts, our resources, our sensitivities. Out of this we gain a sense of the master sentiments and moral examplars by which we desire to be formed over a lifetime.

Each of us must assess the skills we need for that formation, and then seek, with the help of the faith community, to acquire them and practice them. For one person the skill needed may be gratitude; for another repentance and forgiveness; for another the capacity for silence and solitude.

Step by step, we must gradually weed out our self-deceptions and bring our whole lives under the sway of the Christian Story. Spiritual discipline is not an invitation to fixate on self-actualization or to become inordinately preoccupied with the state of our own souls. Neither Paul nor any other biblical writer hinted that spiritual discipline has to do with securing salvation or "getting to Heaven." The sheer irony of spiritual discipline is that it requires our sustained attention, yet attention trained beyond our own selfish needs and onto God's gracious initiative to involve us in the redemption of the world.

WORSHIP: A PATTERN FOR DISCIPLINE

"Assemble the people, men, women, and little ones, and the sojourner within your towns, that they may hear and learn to fear the Lord your God." (Deut. 31:12-13*a*)

The Christian life acquires its motivation and pattern in the liturgy of the congregation. Worship *(leitourgia)*[12] is the work that the generations do together; hence, it is to include women, men, children, and even strangers and sojourners

(Deut. 31:12). The liturgy is the church's living dialogue with God through word, gesture, rite, ritual, silence, and song.

The church is particularly responsible for drawing children and other uninitiated persons into the Story (Exod. 12:24-27). Participation *precedes* understanding! Comprehension unfolds gradually as the Story becomes the world in which we dwell. This is why it does not make sense to disbar children from participating in worship, especially alongside us in the Eucharist.

Lest the church betray its call to inclusiveness, its communal dialogue is to be the work of the whole people of God, with no exclusions. The church today is beginning to recognize, how, historically, it has silenced the voices of women in the dialogue. Women, along with people of color, are struggling to form a redemptive memory by gathering up their experience and their history and joining their voices to the church's living dialogue with God.

Worship begins within the assembly and then is to be stretched over all of life together, becoming a pervasive style of life. Since corporate worship is the heart of Christian spiritual discipline, the key issue is whether or not something redemptive happens to us in worship. Christian formation is the intensely personal yet corporate assimilation of the liturgy. On many levels, the Scripture and tradition implicitly point to the rule: *imitamini quod tractatis*, "imitate what you are handling."

Christian worship, when authentic, is countercultural. It is our way of constructing and living out an alternative vision of reality. We celebrate this radical vision by telling stories of Sarah, Abraham, Isaac, Mary and Joseph, Jesus and Mary, Saint Catherine, Martin Luther King, Mother Teresa, and George Fox.[13] Week after week, our worship challenges the distorted self-understandings imposed on us by our culture and our own personal backgrounds. If worship does not change us, it has not been worship![14]

When worship is authentic, there finally will be no discrepancy between the *shape of the liturgy*, the *shape of community*, and the *shape of our character*. Our work, our *leitourgia*, is to say what we believe and to become what we say.

The shape of the liturgy *is*, therefore, the shape of Christian spirituality. There is a dynamic reciprocity between corporate worship and private devotions. Each nourishes and depends upon the other. The basic dynamics of worship—repentance, confession, praise, proclamation, prayer—provide the basic patterns for a disciplined spiritual life, individual and corporate.

Repentance and Confession

"The time is fulfilled, and the kingdom of God is at hand; repent, and believe in the gospel" (Mark 1:15). Repentance is the threshold for Christian transformation. Repentance is more than feeling remorseful for something we have done. Biblically viewed, repentance is a lifelong turning and returning to God. Becoming Christian requires that we persist in struggling away from the old and toward the new (Rom. 12:2).

Because it is difficult for us to always live up to the claims implicit in our baptism, we repeatedly need to repent. We are stubborn, defiant people, always trying to live self-sufficiently. We are to "turn and become like children" (Matt. 18:3), confessing that we are utterly helpless to *make* ourselves acceptable to God.

Rather than trying to make ourselves into what we are not, repentance depends upon allowing God's grace and mercy to work on us. Only as we surrender and let go of control do we receive from God what we really need in life. Eucharistic liturgy describes the spiritual life as a holy surrender of our selves to God. This requires humility and unqualified trust in God's loyalty to us. We repent by bringing our hopes and desires, our plans and ambitions, our fears and failures, and offering them as a living and holy surrender of ourselves. They are consecrated for service and partnership in God's Realm, made new and given back to us. We are freed to participate with God in joy, freedom, and hope!

Praise and Proclamation

"Praise the Lord! Praise, O servants of the Lord, praise the name of the Lord!" (Psalm 113:1). The spiritual life is rooted in praising and giving thanks to God and in proclaiming God's goodness. Gratitude is our primal response to who God is and what God has done for us (Heb. 12:28). "Thanks *[charis]* be to God for his inexpressible gift" (II Cor. 9:15).

The early Christians partook of the Lord's Supper "with glad and generous hearts, praising God" (Acts 2:46-47*a*). The Greek word *eucharistia* means "joyful thanks" and "gratitude to God." The eucharistic prayers from the early church onward became "great thanksgivings" for all God's redemptive works in creation.

The overwhelming sense of abundant life among both Old and New Testament believers created in them dispositions of effusive gratitude, thanksgiving, praise, and hopefulness. These were more than emotions. Within the New Testament witness, they became liturgical, communal acts (Phil. 4:4; Rom. 12:15; I Thess. 5:16-17; I Tim. 4:4-5). We are called to train our hearts on these dispositions until they become our own characteristic attitudes and affections.

Individuals who are incapable of gratitude and of praising God are incapable of Christian maturity, claims Saliers. In fact, it is irreligious, he adds, to take the world for granted and remain unaffected by both its grandeur and its misery.[15] Barth believed that "radically and basically all sin is simply ingratitude."[16] Gratitude encompasses, rather than ignores or trivializes, the anguish and darkness within human existence. We are called to weep with those who weep and to rejoice with those who rejoice. Yet *in* (not for!) all things, we can give thanks, because nothing can finally separate us from God's love for us in Jesus Christ. Because our lives are filled with pain that strains our sense of gratefulness and tempts us to cynicism and despair, praise and thanksgiving are indeed difficult attitudes. They must be practiced again and again until they become authentic habits of the heart.

Prayer and Meditation

If gratitude is a primal response, then prayer is a primal posture before God. Saliers describes prayer as a way of *intending* the world.[17] To pray with the church is to dialogue with God about the anguish, yearnings, and delights of the world as we know it.

Prayer and meditation transform loneliness into creative solitude. They create space where God may enter and lure us out of self-preoccupation into self-giving. Prayer consists of attention, says Simone Weil, "all the attention of which the soul is capable toward God." To pray is to wait on God to speak.[18] In order to sustain prayer as a way of life, we need to structure time within our lives for daily meditation, periodic spiritual life retreats, and days of recollection.

A major obstacle we face today is hyperactivity. Most of us treat prayer as a dispensable luxury when life gets hectic. To us, time is money, and thus, time spent in prayer and meditation can seem so wasteful. Prayer in fact is noninstrumental in character. It includes a dimension of not-doing that is so difficult for us achievement-addicted Westerners to comprehend.[19] As Gutierrez reminds us, "Prayer is an experience of gratuitousness. This 'leisure' action, this 'wasted' time, reminds us that the Lord is beyond the categories of useful and useless."[20] The creation of space for silence and solitude can seem so outrageous in a world filled with hunger, terrorism, war, and poverty. Yet making time for prayer *is* radical witness in the contemporary hyperactive milieu.

As we journey deeper into Christian existence, prayer becomes a pervasive way of life. Gradually we grow away from immature views of prayer as production, as a pragmatic way to get things done, as a device of self-actualization, as only a means of personal consolation, as a way to rake in personal goodies.

Don Saliers views prayer as the crucible of Christian living. He shows how prayer can become our own living dialogue with God and can teach us to speak to God in praise and gratitude; to look in the direction that God's love is looking; to intercede for the world in all its actuality; to deepen and refine our heartfelt religious affections; to strengthen the connection between what we intend and what we do; to pray with the community of faith, even when alone in our closets; to serve the world by praying for the world; to lead a life of active prayer and prayerful action.

Above All: "Do This . . ."

"Do this in remembrance of me" (Luke 22:19). The Lord's Supper is the paradigm for all our spiritual disciplines, insisted Wesley. In glorious recollection, we celebrate through ritual and symbol the whole sweep of God's saving work, from creation to redemption to anticipation of Christ's coming in final victory (I Cor. 11:26).

If we are to renew spirituality within the congregation, we must center our worship in the Lord's Supper. Because the eucharistic meal is the prefiguration of the Great Banquet that includes those from north, south, east, and west (Luke 13:29; Matt. 8:11), we most visibly are the sign of the world God wills when we express our unity around the table.

During the late Middle Ages, the Eucharist unfortunately

was laden with doleful overtones owing to penitential and sacrificial themes. In terms of contemporary theology, however, the Eucharist is to be offered as our sacrifice *of praise and thanksgiving.* The focus is on the thankful recalling and rehearsing of God's saving acts for all people. The Lord's Supper is to be celebrative and communal, not somber and introspective. It is not a priestly performance to be executed with slick and technical efficiency. It is a festive banquet, like a family reunion gathered around the dining table. In it we are *fed.* It is a joyous celebration of the risen and present Christ, in whose body we now participate: "The cup of blessing which we bless, is it not a participation in the blood of Christ? The bread which we break, is it not a participation in the body of Christ?" (I Cor. 10:16-17).

Through the Eucharist we enter more fully into the company of Jesus and the pattern of his life. The fourfold pattern at the Lord's Table—take, bless, break, and share—provides for us the shape for our Christian existence in the world.[21] As through the ordinary elements of bread and wine, so also through the ordinary stuff of our daily lives can Christ become manifest. We take and offer all that we are, as a gift for God's blessing and consecration. God receives, makes holy, and breaks open our lives for others. As the bread is broken open to be shared, our lives are broken open by the Spirit as a holy surrender of ourselves. We become bread for others and living memories of Jesus Christ in the world.[22]

SUMMARY

Spiritual disciplines aim us toward self-giving love, not self-actualization; toward faithfulness, not effectiveness. Were Mother Teresa aiming for effectiveness, she would not spend time in the streets of Calcutta serving the poor and hungry. She would be out fundraising, enlisting a cadre of fundraising analysts! Instead, she chooses the foolishness of compassion and personal presence.

The question to be put to any practice of spiritual discipline is the question of *adequacy*. Spiritual disciplines authenticate the Christian life when they evoke compassion in us, sensitize us to what God is doing in the world, prompt us to embrace the stranger, inspire in us heartfelt affection for God and neighbor, create in us the capacity for self-giving love, and lead us to authentic self-love. If spiritual discipline does not open us to these qualities of character, we likely are practicing bogus spirituality.

5

Participation: Church as Context

Where and how do we learn the skills required to participate in the coming of God's Realm? Where do we learn to recognize its inbreaking?

The first and most important way we learn is by keeping company with God's people. They have a Story to tell, and they equip us to participate in it. Only through participating in all that the church is and does can we learn the Story that determines Christian self-identity. The most powerful influences on our spirituality are the stories, actions, and affections we share within the faith community. In this chapter, we will explore the church, especially the local congregation, as the decisive context for Christian formation and for initiation into the Realm of God.

THE CHURCH AS THE PEOPLE OF GOD

There are diverse ways to view the church. Since the church is such a vastly complex reality, an exhaustive definition is impossible. We need a variety of images to help us appreciate its mystery and complexity. The New Testament presents us with multiple pictures. As a conservative estimate, says Paul Minear, there are more than eighty New Testament images that refer to the church.[1]

The decisive image, says Minear, is "people of God" (cf. I Pet. 2:9-10), known as the *ecclesia*.[2] *Ecclesia* simply refers to people, a gathered group of believers called the congregation. *Ecclesia* is a way to talk about the interpersonal and relational matrix of the church, whatever institutional forms it may take.[3]

The word *ecclesia* is from a Greek root meaning "to call out." The church is the congregation of those called to be a sign of the world God wills. The distinction between church and world thus lies in the basic posture of persons, some of whom confess "we know we are of God" (I John 5:19), and some of whom do not.

A Letter to the Church

There are few biblical resources more fitting than Ephesians[4] to help us begin to grasp the significance of the church as the context for Christian formation. The most distinctive motif of Ephesians is the church,[5] and a rather high view of the church at that. Here we find themes central to ecclesiology: the household of God, the family of God, the people of God, the body of Christ, the new humanity, the new covenant, the holy temple. Notice how many of these are feminine, inclusive metaphors.

Listen to the theological heart of the Epistle:

Therefore remember that at one time you Gentiles in the flesh, [were] . . . alienated from the commonwealth of Israel, and strangers to the covenants of promise, having no hope and without God in the world. But now in Christ Jesus you who once were far off have been brought near in the blood of Christ. For he is our peace, who has made us both one, and has broken down the dividing wall of hostility. . . . So then you are no longer strangers and sojourners,[6] but you are fellow citizens with the saints and members of the household of God . . . Christ Jesus himself being the chief cornerstone . . . in whom you also are built into it for a dwelling place of God in the Spirit. (Eph. 2:11-14, 19-22)

The claims here are fantastic! These images are world embracing. There are no exclusions. God's unfolding *mysterion* includes the participation of *all* creatures, because Gentiles (that is, all the rest of us) are now received into full membership in God's household.[7] Therefore, Ephesians is a letter to us. All of us are now included in the covenant of promise. Nils Dahl suggests that Ephesians is both a reminder and a congratulation that we belong to a church that, although it includes both bad and good elements, preserves the gospel for our benefit nonetheless.[8] Through the church God provides the resources, the gifts, the leaders, the people, and the talents necessary and ingredient to our transformation.

In this letter the writer insists that God's initiative forms the church. But the church is not the exclusive context where redemptive activity goes on. God's participation in the whole created order is the larger context of our lives. God's household (2:19) or "dwelling place . . . in the Spirit" (2:22) is wherever God chooses to be present and active in creation.

Spirituality, as the writer sees it, is our participation in the mystery of God's creative and redemptive work in the world. But, the writer insists, it is the church *itself*, rather than individual Christians one by one, that is being built into that work (2:22). The faith community *as a whole* is being drawn into God's purposes and plans. As the church we are to "make all [creatures] see what is the plan of the mystery hidden for ages in God who created all things; that *through the church* the manifold wisdom of God might now be made known" (Eph. 3:9-10, italics mine).

The church itself is being built into God's activity in the world for the sake of the world. It is none other than the church that brings us within sight of this mystery. The writer tells us that *through the church* and owing to the church we are inescapably involved in what God is doing in the world. Something already is happening! It has been going on from the very beginning (Eph. 1:4-6). We are not striking up anything new. Rather, we are, as the church, learning how to get in on it.

THE CHURCH AS EVENT

Speaking the truth in love, we are to grow up in every way into him who is the head, into Christ, from whom the whole body, joined and knit together . . . makes bodily growth and upbuilds itself in love. (Eph. 4:15-16)

In classical Greek, the verb "to grow" is transitive, as in "to grow a garden." Ephesians puts emphasis upon the church's responsibility for its own growth, not as an automatic or natural process but through spiritual discipline. What is the church to grow into? Being itself! The writer emphasizes the church not as a sociological entity but as a spiritual event.[9] The church is not now fully what it is called to be; it is responsible for becoming so.

Ephesians presents several distinctive understandings of spiritual growth. First, the spiritual growth of the whole faith community is declared decisive, not the spiritual growth of individual Christians. That's quite startling! But Christian spiritual formation fundamentally depends upon a church that is itself alive and caught up into God's creative and redemptive work. The more authentic the experience of the church *as* church, the more authentic will be the experience of Christians who are shaped through initiation and involvement there.

Next, the growth spoken of does not refer to numerical increase or even to strengthened personal faith. It means the deepening of the church's capacity to love as God loves. To grow spiritually is to deepen our partnership, *as the church,* with a God who knits us into a community whose love knows no limits and has no walls.

As we can see, the very character of the church is a continuing task. Whatever the church is, something has to happen. Contemporary ecclesiology is now speaking of the church as *event.* The church is viewed as a continuing project accomplished in particular times by particular people, responding to particular situations. The church is defined in terms of what the church *does.*[10]

God holds the church accountable for becoming the church (I Pet. 4:17). Whatever is supposed to happen comes with no guarantee that it will. Sometimes it does not. Always in the process of being reformed *(ecclesia semper reformanda),* the church is both gift and task. All this adds to the fact that we must talk more about the church in its empirical, everyday reality.

THE CHURCH IN THE SPIRIT

Grace was given to each of us . . . to equip the saints for the work of ministry, for building up the body of Christ. (Eph. 4:7*a*, 12)

The faith community is where the Spirit distributes gifts for Christian vocation in the world. The church is by definition a charismatic community, and in this sense every Christian believer is a charismatic. *Charisms* ("gifts") apply to all baptized believers since "each has his own special gift from God, one of one kind and one of another" (I Cor. 7:7).

New Testament writers were far more interested in a sociology than a psychology of Spirit! Everything they taught about gifts of the Spirit stands over against prevalent attitudes of individualism and privatism. No spiritual gift is given for use only in one's own private journey. The greatest spiritual gifts are those that edify the whole believing community

(I Cor. 14:2-12; Eph. 4:12). Paul insists that we use our gifts "to excel in building up the Church" (I Cor. 14:12).

Unfortunately, we have kept the Spirit too much tied to the interiority of the individual believer. Therefore, when Paul suggests that "you are God's temple" and that "God's Spirit dwells in you" (I Cor. 3:16), we automatically assume that Paul means in each one of us individually. Yet when we listen very carefully, we are in for a surprise! Paul does not begin with the individual person. He begins with the church. To say that the Spirit dwells in us means in our faith community. When a profound sense of community is lost, then spirituality implies nothing beyond the private zones of existence. Barth reminds us: Christian existence is very personal, but it is not a private matter![11]

The nature of the Spirit does not lie in substance but in relationship. The church uses the symbol of the Trinity to suggest that God's own self is expressed in communal, relational terms. God, three *persons* in one, displays perfect mutuality and unity. God's triune reality shows us the profound mystery of relating for the very sake of that which is other. This is to be the shape of life in the faith community.

The primary work of the Spirit in the church, then, is to bestow participation in a form of life (I Pet. 4:10-11). Within the community of Spirit we glimpse, however imperfectly, the breaking open of qualities that identify the Spirit among us: mutuality, interdependency, creativity, freedom, service, witness.

THE CHURCH: REDEMPTIVE?

While a doctoral student at Princeton Theological Seminary, I presented a paper in our practical theology seminar on the formative power of the congregation. Here I was speaking of its power to initiate us into the Christian faith and there nurture and sustain us through the twists and turns of life's experience. I spoke of the redemptive power of the people of God and of their promise, upon the baptism of each one of us into the household of faith, to help our families bring us up in the Christian faith. I thought that in certain portions of the paper, at least, I had waxed lofty and profound on ecclesiology.

Present in our seminar was Heije Faber, a practical theologian and visiting scholar from Holland. When I finished reading my paper, he caught my attention. With subtle drama he closed my paper and laid it aside, folded his hands together, leaned across the table, peered over his glasses, and said, "Now, let's talk about the church as you and I *really* know it!"

Instantly I knew what he meant. Frankly, I had realized while writing the paper that the experience of many people, myself included, did not altogether match up with my sudden flourish of ecclesiology. In my attention to the theologically normative character of the church, I neglected to reflect much on the empirical church as you and I know it through our own involvements.

Our experience in the faith community over the course of a lifetime *does* have a profound formative and redemptive effect. But this is not all. On occasion, we are hurt rather than healed by our church involvements. Sometimes our congregations seem to be microcosms of the predominating culture rather than countercultural, healing communities. Rather than drawing us nearer to God, to self, and to others, at times the church alienates us. It can be slow to embrace persons who are different and quick to be judgmental and self-righteous.

Important to the spiritual vitality of the church are honest images and self-understandings. Pseudo-images will suffocate the church and its redemptive, shaping power in our lives. The church actually exists in a dialectical tension between its theologically normative character and its concrete, everyday reality. Most longtime churchgoers know that their experience of this or that congregation does not altogether match the normative descriptions of the church found in our systematic theology textbooks.

The character of the church is the same as that of an individual Christian, a justified sinner *(simul iustus et peccator)*. Like the individual, says Howard Grimes, the church is both redeemed and *being* redeemed. There is always a tension between what the church is and what it may become.[12] As Craig Dykstra comments, the church "like all the world, has lived and continues to live unredemptively, nearsightedly and half-blindedly, sinfully."[13]

With this in mind, two basic theological realities are central to understanding the church as decisive for Christian formation. Here I take my lead from Dykstra's perceptive comments in an article on the formative power of the congregation.[14] The first claim is that when we are involved in the church, we are caught up together into mutually reinforced patterns of self-destruction. The second claim is that within the church these patterns are being modified and their destructive effects transformed.

The church, local and universal, is caught up into powerful and profound patterns of alienation and self-destruction. At times these patterns make us physically sick. They surely make us emotionally and spiritually sick. Yet transformation happens within as well as despite this very context! Through the church's witness, time and again we experience redemption and release from mutual and self-destruction.

What do we mean by "patterns of self-destruction," and what are specific examples of this? The achievement-oriented and competitive lifestyle described by social psychologists is a pervasive pattern of self-destruction in our culture. Achievement addiction is socially structured, socially mediated and mutually reinforced early in American life. Deeply engrained in our cultural ethos and reinforced at every level of society, even young children and adolescents suffer from it. What is the achievement orientation? In the words of Dykstra, "the achievement-oriented lifestyle is a style of life which has as its center the *compulsion* to succeed or achieve in whatever social world one lives. . . . Who one is, one's identity, depends upon *earning* the affection of others through the value of what one produces or does. This compulsion to achieve affects, almost to the point of determining, one's behavior, attitudes, values, and fundamental beliefs."[15]

In his book *The Hurried Child,* clinical child psychologist David Elkind documents the destructive effects of achievement addiction on American children. Research indicates that suicide victims often are high achievers in school. Many adolescents are caught up into "achievement overload" by academic, interpersonal, and extracurricular demands placed on them. "When young people assume that parents are concerned only with how well they do rather than with who they are, the need to achieve becomes addictive."[16]

A female pastor I know tells of a dream that, to her horror, revealed just how deeply she had internalized the compulsion to achieve and produce. The dream came during a period when she was experiencing painful physical symptoms— muscle spasms in her back and neck, arms and legs, which gripped and clenched her whole body in pain.

In the dream, she found herself standing on the threshold of a room filled with little girls. Each little girl was sick or maimed in some pitiful way. One was missing her arms. The most vivid image in the dream was a girl confined to a chair, the lower half of her body missing. She sat at a machine that she had to crank by hand, round and round, day and night. It was a life support machine; if she stopped cranking it, she would die.

My friend did not readily understand the dream. Who were these little girls? Who or what maimed them so horribly?

The coincidence of the dream during the period of painful physical symptoms prompted her to go to a Jungian dream analyst. (She also went to a doctor for a physical exam.)

As she sat before the therapist and narrated the dream, she broke down in tears but still did not know why it made her feel so bad. When she finished her account, the therapist leaned forward and asked, "Tell me, where is this chair and this desk at which *you* sit?" The light suddenly dawned! As she and the analyst worked on it, the dream became obvious: The little girls were parts of herself, tyrannized by the incessant compulsion to produce and the addiction to achieve. The conviction that her self-esteem and self-worth were predicated on production and achievement was maiming her deeply within.

This woman had internalized at the deepest levels of her psyche the message that her self-worth derives singularly from what she *does* rather than who she *is*. She was physically ill, emotionally hurting, and spiritually diseased by the compulsion to produce and achieve.

When we so deeply buy into the achievement motive and the system it generates, Dykstra notes, we largely forfeit the one thing on which we most fundamentally depend as human beings: the giving and receiving of unconditional love. Each of us longs for ascriptive, not achieved, worth. That is, we cry out to be loved just for *being* here, not for what we can produce or achieve. We yearn to be known, valued, and loved as an unrepeatable, precious child of God. The irony is that the profound experience of ascriptive love sets us free to be the best we can be.

The achievement motive is so mutually destructive, furthermore, because we feel forced to hide from one another. We convince ourselves that we cannot be loved just as we are, with all our fears, failures, and faults. So we are driven to earning love, to modeling effectiveness rather than faithfulness, to achieving no matter the cost, to projecting a public persona rather than revealing a real person. Eventually, the cost is high and heavy. We become, as Dykstra alludes, persons who are tense, manipulative, deceptive, controlling, competitive, and cruel to ourselves and to one another.

What are some other patterns—mutually reinforced and socially celebrated—by which we wreak destruction on ourselves? Clericalism, classism, racism, and sexism are all patterns we daily experience and subtly reinforce that diminish us and make us sick people. The final outcome is that on frequent occasion we utterly and mutually fail one another and ourselves. Therefore, as Dykstra points out, the source of our spiritual sustenance must come from beyond one another.

Through the witness of the faith community we come to know the Everlasting One who never fails, who never is absent, and who wills more good for us than we do for ourselves. God's love is the power that redeems our failures of one another. While our tendency to self-alienation is profound and real, what is also real and true is that we are, as members of the community of faith, caught up into profound and powerful patterns of redemption and transformation.

Were it not for our worship of God, life in the faith community would be nothing more than participation in just another sociological group that subtly engages in self-destruction. Worship of God slices through our self-destructiveness.[17] In worship of God alone lies our freedom from achievement addiction, from self-disgust, from self-aggrandizement, from self-righteousness, from disappointment in one another. In a lifestyle of authentic worship of God, suggests Dykstra, there is considerable, yet not always perfect, freedom from the self-destructive effects of these patterns. They are redemptively modified, though in this lifetime not completely eliminated from our existence.

THE CHURCH AS THE FAMILY OF GOD

And [Jesus] replied, "Who are my mother and my brothers?" And looking around on those who sat about him, he said, "Here are my mother and my brothers! Whoever does the will of God is my brother, and sister, and mother." (Mark 3:33-35)

The church redemptive is the "family of God," another decisive, feminine metaphor for the church. The church is not essentially an institution; it is a family, a community, a gathered people. To be baptized is to be reborn into a new, all-inclusive family. Jesus said, "Whoever loves God is my family."

To be baptized means to accept the family of God as the primary formative environment for oneself or one's child. The church is to understand itself as a family not defined by bloodlines or biology but by common participation in the ministry of Jesus Christ. Baptism is a radical commitment that, in fact, puts the church family *before* the biological family (Luke 14:26). It may even set a believer at odds with the biological or nuclear family (Matt. 10:34-39). Stanley Hauerwas concludes, therefore, that the first task of the church in regard to the family is to be a community that claims loyalty and significance beyond the family.[18]

As John Westerhoff observes, the modern family is slowly being dispossessed of its traditional functions.[19] Hence, more than ever before, believers need for the church to recover its radical identity as the family of God. The church is to be our fundamental social unit for living and our basic source of self-identity as persons. The faith community must transform our experience of family, not the other way around!

To be family means to provide an appropriate, interpersonal, relational environment so as to empower, nourish, and sustain formation of Christian character. Family is a character-forming environment. It is where we can nourish uniqueness and individuality without slipping into undue privatism and individualism.

The family of faith gathers as a *reconciling* household, rather than as one already reconciled. Here we learn, albeit slowly and painfully, to share life redemptively. We show up just as we are to find out what redemption means and to acquire the skills to live redemptively in the world.

To become a "family-oriented congregation" does not mean, therefore, to focus particularly on the biological nuclear family, though in contemporary society it needs all the support we can give it. It means, rather, to embrace one another—whether single or married or divorced, whether black or yellow or brown, whether female or male, whether young or old, whether rich or poor—as family, and to live with familial commitments toward one another. So then, we are no longer strangers; we are family!

The Family Welcomes Strangers

When we become members of the family of faith, we inherit a family tradition with which we must come to terms for the rest of our lives. Membership here constantly demands that we enlarge our sense of who belongs. The broken wall (Eph. 2:13), says Markus Barth, means the end of every sort of exclusion and ghetto.[20] The family of God, thus, is not a football draft. We do not get to pick and choose who is on our team.

In important ways the faith community is *unlike* our modern conception of the family. We approach the family today as a utopian retreat from the outside, a castle of comfort, an escape from the public. It is not fitting, however, to view the church simply as an harmonious haven of like-minded people. Christian spirituality includes both comfort and discomfort, the familiar and the strange. The faith community is where we spend ourselves as well as recollect and replenish ourselves.

Christian existence means freedom to embrace the other as family member. This does not simply mean freedom for other believers like us, that is, those already in the faith community. It means freedom for *all* others, freedom for all those whom God creates and loves. We are called actively to search out the poor, the different, the dispossessed. Now, living under a new covenant, we are called to see them as fellow creatures and fellow sufferers. The writer of Hebrews urges us, for instance, to "remember those who are in prison, *as though* in prison with them; and those who are ill-treated" (Heb. 13:3, italics mine).

Conversion to God is always coincidental with conversion to welcoming the stranger (Heb. 13:3; I Pet. 4:9), as well as loving the neighbor (Mark 12:28-34; Rom. 13:8). Time and again biblical writers decry bogus spirituality that claims love of God yet ignores the neighbor and provides no hospitality to the stranger (cf. I John 4:20; James 2:14-17). The company of God's people was always admonished to include the company of strangers and sojourners (Exod. 22:21; Deut. 10:19).

Though mutuality, forgiveness, and *agape* love are part of the distinctive experience of the family of God, the decisive thing about it is its startling redefinition of the status of the stranger.[21] In fact, John Koenig insists that hospitality to strangers is the hermeneutical key to the entire biblical witness.[22]

What is hospitality? It is the creation of an environment or space where the stranger is welcomed and received as gift, blessing, and fellow creature, rather than treated as threat, intruder, or annoyance. Hospitality means open doors, open hearts, open classrooms, open lives. We make our very selves present and available to the other, so that we may mutually discover and receive the potential gifts one another have to bear.

Who are the strangers we are to welcome? They are people like us and unlike us. They are our children and our rebellious adolescents. They are the people whose presence embarrasses us, the crippled, the unbathed, the uneducated, the mentally retarded; those whose ways confuse or alienate us, or threaten or offend us. We can welcome and embrace them not because we have any particular warm, fuzzy feelings for them but simply because, through the covenant of promise, we can see them as our own fellow sufferers in Jesus Christ.

If we focus, then, on creating and enjoying intimacy with one another *to the exclusion* of creating space for the stranger to enter, we forfeit our own participation in the covenant of Christ. Strangers are not merely occasions for doing good and feeling good; they are our fellow creatures, and children of the God we worship.

The Family Is a Community of Equals

Inasmuch as it incorporates us into a community living under the commandment to radical equality, hospitality, and inclusiveness, baptism is the foe of any form of exclusion from the church's worship, witness, and work. Baptism is the sacrament of radical equality.[23] The strongest statements of equality in the New Testament occur in the context of baptismal liturgy (Gal. 3:27-28).

In baptismal waters, all human distinctions that keep us unequal are washed away! Baptism proclaims freedom, mutuality, and shared leadership. Through baptism we each are ordained into the priesthood of all believers, disallowing any clerical or gender bias to the ministry of the church. The practice of denying ordination to women on account of their sexual gender, as White argues, implicitly repudiates the validity of their baptism.[24] If the baptismal liturgy is true, then many problems related to justice owe to our failure to appropriate the gifts and demands of our baptism.

Though the primitive church reflected the radical vision of equality revealed in Jesus, the later church instead proposed a definition of community and leadership unfortunately gleaned from cultural patriarchy. However, the model of power for Christians, as Russell points out, is God's self-presentation in Jesus Christ, where lordship and servanthood stand in dynamic paradox. Accordingly, our own power relationships must exist in the same paradoxical tension.[25] Leadership and power within the community of faith really can, under the influence of the Spirit, be fluid and shared, without resort to hierarchy and domination. As a prefigurative community and enclave of the future,[26] the church is called to be a family that displays radical equality.

THE ECCLESIAL SHAPE OF SPIRITUALITY

As we can see, it is impossible to talk about Christian formation and Christian spirituality without talking about the church. This chapter has sought to build a case for the ecclesial shape of Christian spirituality.

The faith community is not only the decisive *context* for Christian spirituality, it is the very *shape* of our spiritual existence. To become a Christian is to enter and to participate in a historical, corporate Way of life together. Through the *ecclesia*, God introduces us to the relational, interdependent, and thus truly human existence for which we were created. In this context alone are our lives altered *toward* redemption. The old life is mixed with the new, to be sure, and so we constantly need forgiveness from one another and from God.

It is important, therefore, not to treat the church simply as a voluntary resource for our respective spiritual journeys. The life of the faith community *is* the shape of the journey. Christian spirituality is irreducibly communal, liturgical, relational, and sacramental, as well as deeply personal.

SUMMARY

It is only as the church is alive to participation in the creative and redemptive work of God that it can be a community that forms Christian character. Through the church our sphere of participation is enlarged, clarified, deepened, and revealed finally to be much larger than we ever dreamed. This is the focus of Christian educational ministry.

Where we find the church becoming itself, we find a community of lived faith where persons welcome strangers as bearing potential gifts; a community where diversity is celebrated and not looked upon as annoyance or threat; a community that nourishes individuality, avoiding both excess individualism and excess conformism; a community that provides equal access to leadership; a community that repents, prays, and praises together. This is the shape of life in the Realm of God!

Above all, we find a church that has learned how to catch believers up into the drama of Christian Story, its promise, challenges, and surprises. It is to that Story that we now turn our attention.

6

Participation: Story as Content

Human beings are born storytellers. To become a Christian is to enter, to live, to tell a particular story. The church is where we are introduced to the old, old Story, decisive for Christian existence in the contemporary world.

We go to church to hear its Story and to be changed by hearing. By repeatedly dramatizing the plot, by introducing us to all the characters, by telling us the many twists and turns, the church draws us into the ongoing Story as participants ourselves. It teaches us how to negotiate the hows and what-nexts, the surprises, struggles, and victories of the radical, countercultural way of life that Christianity is.

WE ARE STORIED PEOPLE

"To be a person is to have a story."[1] Many theologians today suggest that human character is best understood as formed, as unfolded, and as revealed in narrative. We live in narrative as fish in water! For that reason, it is difficult for us to see the profound importance of narrative to our sense of self and world. We are apt to think of story simply as an artistic device. Story is more than this. Narrative is the primordial way we talk about and mediate our experience. We dream and daydream in narrative, remember, anticipate, hope, despair, believe, doubt, plan, gossip, hate, and love in narrative.[2]

When we remember, we do so in narrative. Yet our past is not a storehouse of unalterable facts, that is, what happened when.[3] The past is a story we tell and retell, first in this way and then in that. We do all kinds of things and feel all kinds of things about our past. Yet we always live in the hope that a truer way to remember and to tell our story may break in upon us. For the Christian, that is the moment of metanoia, or conversion. The question, then, is not whether but *how* we tell our story. "Even the unexamined life, the 'drifter,'" says Ann Brennan, "is living a powerful story of 'Storylessness.'"[4]

Self-identity and character, therefore, are essentially autobiographical and narrative in nature. There is no other way to reveal who we are without telling our story. Our individual life stories reveal what we have done in order to come up with a certain kind of self. Our character is rooted in story, unfolded through story, and changed through story. Story gives material content to our character. We not only shape but are also shaped by the stories we choose to tell about ourselves. Who am I? "A wandering Aramean was my father . . ." We are stories unfolding through time.

STORY: A METAPHOR FOR REALITY

What do we mean by "story?" Gabriel Fackre defines narrative theologically as "an account of characters and events in a plot moving over time and space through conflict toward resolution."[5] Through storytelling we draw certain connections between the onrush of life events, in order to orient ourselves in one way or another to those events. In this way, the flow of life becomes a plot marked by a storyline. Theologically speaking, we struggle to see events as patterned according to an unfolding divine purpose, not merely occurring randomly or meaninglessly.

The structure of narrative is not the exact structure of reality nor identical with it, yet narrative is a primary way we mediate and express our sense of reality. Put another way, we use story as an extended metaphor for reality.

Stories reveal actions and the responses of individuals and groups. Inasmuch as intention-action constitutes who we are and not merely illustrates, stories shape and reveal our character as we become committed to *this* course of action rather than *that* course. Hauerwas suggests, therefore, that the soul of narrative is not, as we commonly think, the plot. It is, rather, the unfolding of human character as people, circumstances, and events interact.

SCRIPTURE AND TRADITION: A VAST STORY!

Story is integral to Christian discourse. We are a storied people because the God who creates us is a storied God. Elie Wiesel suggests that God created us because God likes good stories!

Our shared memory as Christians is narrative in character. The Judeo-Christian tradition is a particular Story with a particular plot and particular events, characters, times, and places. Christianity is a form as well as a message; it is a narrative.[6] To call Christianity a story is *not*, of course, to call it fictitious. Though the Judeo-Christian Story is not essentially an empirical recounting, it does include history and presupposes "reality out there" (ontological) truth claims.

As constitutive of the faith community, the Story was eventually set forth in writings that evolved into Scripture or canon, taken to be apostolic. Karl Barth viewed Scripture as "one vast, loosely structured non-fictional novel."[7] That is, the diverse materials of scripture, whether poetic, prophetic, legal, liturgical, or historical, are all embraced in one long, overarching Story.[8]

The metaphor of Christian Story includes not only Scripture but also tradition. As an ingenious mingling of history and nonhistory, experience and interpretation, into one long, continuous story,[9] tradition refers both to the *activity* of handing on the gospel and to *that which* is handed on.

Christian Story, thus, means much more than simple narrative. It is a way to talk about the entire Christian witness of faith. The good news is a dynamic story transcending any written texts, whose final outcome is yet to be written in or beyond history. The Story is expressed not only through Scripture, but also through liturgy, sacraments, symbols, rituals, creeds, doctrines, holy artifacts, practices of piety, and many other means.

Scripture itself presents its own means for teaching, preaching, and initiating persons into the Story: parables, poetry, proverbs, prayers, liturgies, laments, metaphors, symbols, songs, stories of ordinary people. Rather than chopping Scripture into morsels of information to be dispensed in preaching and teaching, we can take our clues for communicating the Story from the multiple dramatic as well as didactic forms in which it comes to us.

LISTENING TO STORIES

Christians are shaped by three basic texts of story: (1) life story, (2) cultural story, and (3) Christian Story. An important subtext is the particular congregation and denomination that mediates the Christian Story to us. Christian education is that dimension of the church's ministry that seeks to bring these stories into conversation, one with another. The aim is not only to reflect upon, to interpret, and to understand them, but also to critically test and revise them. The ultimate aim, however, is to be moved to worship and to praise the Eternal One whose presence is revealed in them.

"Listening" others into speaking, and into telling their stories (Nelle Morton) is thus an important task of educational ministry. We are called to help persons tell, interpret, and then retell their stories in light of the Christian Story. This ministry requires that in working with persons we (1) listen and accept unconditionally their life stories; (2) invite them to reflect upon and to bring their stories into dialogue with the Christian Story; (3) empower their stories to be interpreted by and caught up into the Christian Story; and (4) help them to negotiate the Story in their own unique life contexts.

CHRISTIAN STORY
AND CHRISTIAN EDUCATION

Christianity is not, as we have alluded, a piece of historical information that the church can purvey to new initiates. It is a self-involving Story that makes claims upon its hearers.

The Bible, as interpreted by specific faith traditions, is the primary resource for telling and retelling the Judeo-Christian Story. As the key resource for worship, for instruction, and for devotion by Christian believers, the Bible is at the heart of the church. From birth to death, the Bible accompanies members of the faith community, even if given individual Christians never open it up and read it for themselves.

Worship is for most Christians the place where the Scriptures are heard and assimilated on a regular and lifelong basis. In worship, the Bible is read, sung, prayed and preached, then sometimes carried home for personal devotions or group study.

There exists today, however, a widespread recognition of the loss of the Bible within the church, accompanied by growing efforts to reclaim its centrality in worship and in education.[10] Phyllis Bird attributes the Bible's silence to the loss of its credibility in the modern world. Recovery of the Bible cannot be obtained simply by reasserting its authority or by redoubling efforts to teach and preach it. The key lies in *how* we approach the Scriptures. The Bible's authority, suggests Bird, will be restored only "when it is read and heard in such a way that it provides the determinative story and symbols and references for Christian self-understanding, for worship, for theological discourse, and for engagement with the world."[11]

The Bible, as a key witness to faith, does not just lie there inertly. It can exert tremendous life-changing power on us. We not only read and interpret the Bible, the Bible interprets us! It *does* things to us, for us, among us. Hence, we sense that through the Bible we encounter the living Word of God, God's own self-revelation through Israel and in Jesus Christ. As Walter Brueggemann notes, "One does not need to be magical, supernaturalist, or superstitious to argue that this literature proceeds with a discernible power and intentionality that impinges upon and shatters all old descriptions of reality and invites one into a differently described reality."[12]

For a large segment of Christians, unfortunately, the Bible remains in the remote past because in the Protestant church it has been assigned a burden of false expectations.[13] As Bird points out, we sometimes tell ourselves that the Bible is simple, straightforward, easy to comprehend, and needing no interpretation. The Bible is the church's greatest treasure, but in fact, it is complex and difficult to understand.

The Bible is not a self-interpreting book. To enter its Story and make it our own entails an encounter with the strange and unfamiliar. It is to enter into the experience of others who have gone before us. Their world, however, is distant and alien from our own, in time, space, culture, language, and self-understanding.

The Story the Bible mediates can become our story only as we preach, teach, study, ponder, meditate, question, probe, and dialogue around it *within* the community of faith.

When we set out to journey into the biblical Story, we need to make preparations; we need traveling companions, guidance, openness, anticipation. Not the least, we need to practice personal and corporate spiritual disciplines, since they posture our bodies and our souls rightly to *hear* the Story, *say* the Story, *do* the Story, and *be* the Story together.[14]

WE READ THE STORY

In *Called to Freedom*, Daniel Migliore shows how the Bible is to be read essentially as the Story of God's liberation of those in bondage (Exod. 20:2). The Story depicts the astonishing freedom of God for us. God is on the side of life! God is the advocate and author of genuine freedom *from* all bondage and *for* abundant living.

The hermeneutical key for Christian education, consequently, lies in how well we read, interpret, and proclaim the Scriptures as a message that liberates persons from negation as sacred and inviolable children of God. Recovering the Bible as a liberating word also means uncovering its cultural captivity. There are five ways (at least!) in which the Bible is held captive today: biblicism, historicism, psychologism, privatism, and objectivism.[15]

1. Biblicism. Biblicism refers to a distorted understanding of what it means to call the Bible the Word of God. For some this means claiming the supernatural origin of Scripture or the infallibility and inerrancy of Scripture in order to protect Scripture's authority. Scriptural authority does not rest in the words themselves, however. Luther and Calvin recognized the Bible as a human document, the words of Scripture alone being neither inspired nor authoritative.[16] The Word of God is expressed in Jesus Christ, not in a collection of writings.

Scripture as Word of God is derivative. The Bible itself is not the Word but is a primary witness to it. A witness does not call attention to itself, but rather points beyond!

2. Historicism. The liberating power of modern historical-critical scholarship cannot be overestimated. It contributed much to unlocking the Bible for Christians. Yet it unfortunately also led to some shortcomings. The interest of historians turned to establishing "what really happened" (the facts and events behind the text), leading to a separation of the Bible from its literary form. Hans Frei refers to this as the "eclipse of biblical narrative." The upshot was to create distance between text and hearer, locating authority in the accuracy of factual reports of the past. Today biblical scholars agree that the scientific, historical method *alone* is not enough. They now draw from hermeneutics (the science of interpretation) as well as literary approaches that help us attend to the textual narrative, to the plot, and to the character that people develop as they undergo God.[17]

3. Psychologism. One reaction to the distance created by the historical-critical method is to debunk tradition and history and sink into the "warm stream of immediate experience."[18] But when overpsychologized, the scriptures are robbed of their historical bite. The key is to blend objective and subjective approaches to Bible study so that the approach is of one piece, avoiding psychological or historical or any other form of reductionism. Thomas Groome's "shared praxis" approach, for instance, emphasizes a praxis methodology, bringing present lived experience—in specific sociocultural contexts—into critical engagement with biblical texts.[19]

4. Privatism. Lacking communal guidance, psychologism leads to isolated and private interpretations of the biblical texts. When approached through the extreme individualism that is so insidious in modern culture, the story of God's "for us" work in Jesus Christ is eclipsed by an overriding "for me" attitude. Little or no attention is given to the corporate character of liberation and salvation.

5. Objectivism. Here we confront the myth of objective interpretation of scripture, or else the impression given by some evangelists that the Bible can be presented straightforwardly with utterly no interpretation. Modern hermeneutical theory demonstrates, to the contrary, that any given reading of any text is influenced by what is brought to it. When we interpret, or even when we simply *read* the Bible, we are influenced by subjective, conscious, and unconscious concerns that we bring with us. When claims are made to an objective, value-neutral position, therefore, we can safely guess that they are made by persons in power who claim the right to adjudicate what is *the* consensus view and what is deviant from it.

THE STORY READS US

Christian education involves bringing before us life and cultural and biblical texts to interpret. But it does not stop there. We read and interpret the Story, but it also interprets us! The Story does not just sit there, it does something to *us*. The Story intends to qualify us to think, to feel, to act in new ways.[20] As the Story is told and proclaimed, one does not agree or disagree with the Story: One is affected or one is not.[21] Upon its impact we become different; we feel changed, renewed, restored, transformed.

Scripture creates its own particular world and domain of meaning. One task of Christian education is to extend this meaning over the whole of reality.[22] Let us notice the direction of relating our own stories and the Christian Story. The invitation is not that we find *our* story in the Bible.

Rather, it is that we make God's Story, as attested in Scripture, our own story.[23]

The Story, when retold and taught in ways fitting to both its content *and* its form, does many things to us. It creates a world, structures our consciousness, suggests attitudes and actions, directs our attention in this way and that, encourages particular values, invites certain commitments, evokes feelings, provokes a new social imagination. The authority of the Bible owes, at least in part, to what its witness *does* to its hearers. That is, its authority is functional.

The Story Renders the Character of God

Christianity is not a self-help, self-improvement program for which spirituality is but the latest technique. It is a Story that intends to render to us the character of the God we worship. In its bare bones, the storyline is of a God who creates, reconciles, and redeems the world.[24] The Bible speaks mainly not of God's attributes but of God's actions. It reveals who God is by narrating what God does (Deut. 10:17-18). It also tells us how reality is to be construed and life to be lived in light of God's character, depicted in the stories of Israel and Jesus.[25]

God is presented not only as chief actor but also as author of the Story. The Story reveals who God is and what God does with ordinary human beings like you and me in our ordinary lives. We are shown how character is both evoked and revealed as we participate with God redemptively in the world. Perhaps our image and likeness to God, suggests William Bausch, resides in our being paragraphs to God's story.[26]

The Story Changes Us

From the outset, the Story demands a decision, makes a claim, and evokes a response. The Story presupposes that we will be changed and in fact must be changed in order to be partners in God's work. We may call the change conversion or a born-again experience. Or the change may be a matter of moving from nominal to deeper participation in God's redemptive work. "Growth" and "development" are not entirely adequate ways of describing the changes wrought by the jarring impact of the Story. Change characteristically is wrenched from us, and often comes with pain, discontinuity, disorientation.

The Story intends to have a deeply personal effect, aiming not to reduce tension but to heighten and focus it! It does this by revealing how, without God, we labor under the logic of self-defeat. It exposes our brokenness and reveals the false hopes that we bring into our relationship with God in the first place. Then it sets our hearts on a new and startling way of looking at reality. In and through the Story, we claim to find the courage and the skill to confess the evil that we do.[27] Permitting us to see ourselves as unrelentlessly loved and known by God, it reminds us that God's grace is the most fundamental reality of our lives.

The Story Mediates a New World

The Bible is like a script for shaping our imaginations and perceptions in ways so decisive that we forever view our world and ourselves through lenses that this script supplies.[28] The Story serves not only to establish a new world but also to orient us morally and ethically within it. "What is moral is *not* 'self-evident,' as Freud declared in a letter to James Putnam. What is moral becomes and remains self-evident only within a powerful and deeply compelling system of culture."[29] The Christian Story structures for us such a powerful and deeply compelling sense of reality. Becoming Christian is much more than gaining a Weltanschaaung ("world view").

Christianity is a Way of living that correlates seeing with doing, hearing with obeying.

The Story Subverts the Old World

Christian Story establishes us in a new world and new self-identity by subverting the old. The parables of Jesus, for instance, are assaults on our conventional and taken-for-granted sense of reality. They break through the social and mythic structures that we build for our comfort and security.[30] The encounter that explodes out of the parabolic stories is none other than the Realm of God. Parables are pictures of persons who encounter the New Age, showing the kind of character they develop when they choose to participate in its coming.

The new world given by God is more than an existential, psychological, or spiritual reality. It also has to do with public, communal, corporate structures of living. The call to the Realm of God is the call to embrace a covenantal mode of life. Since reality is socially constructed and not simply given, then it may be undone and in fact must be dismantled in order to make room for the new world.

Conversion to God's Realm necessarily sets us at odds with present social arrangements that serve the interests of a selected few at the expense of a majority of others. To tell the Story is to be thrust into an ongoing critique of all that is illegitimate in the old world, and into refusing ill-gotten power and wealth.

The Story Mediates Hope and Promise

"My grief is beyond healing, my heart is sick within me" (Jer. 8:18). The Christian Story opens us to the reality of pain and suffering and to the power of evil within human existence. Not pain and suffering itself but the despairing sense of being "beyond healing" is the sway of evil in our lives. Most secular stories are calculated to trivialize evil or to treat it as a noncategory. The Christian Story claims that evil is real, powerful, and as costly as the cross of Christ. Through the Story we experience the reversal of influences that invite disbelief and despair. We are given promise and hope.

Glib certitude is not Christian hope. Christian hope is in fact a "dialogue with despair,"[31] emerging only on the far side of despair. For "we know that the whole creation has been groaning in travail together until now; and not only the creation, but we ourselves" (Rom. 8:22-23). Where is God while babies die like flies because they have no food? Where is God when innocent bystanders are maimed daily at the hands of vicious terrorists? Where is God when innocent people are victimized in their own homes and neighborhoods? Where is God when black people are tortured, killed, and silenced daily in South Africa? Where was God in Auschwitz?

The Story gives us the language by which to cry out to God in our pain. Scripture, in fact, prompts us to get in touch with our real pain in the first place. It helps sustain us not by conveying a philosophy of suffering and evil but rather through its witness that "none of us lives to himself, and none of us dies to himself. If we live, we live to the Lord, and if we die, we die to the Lord; so then, whether we live or whether we die, we are the Lord's" (Rom. 14:7-8).

GUIDELINES TO READING

Our clear calling today is to recover a teaching office centered in Scripture, using tradition, reason, and, in particular, experience in ways that keep and tell a liberating Story, a Story that lends meaning to modern existence. For those who "love to tell the Story," guidelines are needed to help overcome the eclipse of the biblical narrative. The following are suggestive, not exhaustive.

1. First, we can read the Bible *contextually*. As we noticed, the activity of interpretation is inseparable from a particular situation in life. However objective we may think we are, we always read and interpret Scripture with interests and presuppositions that owe to our particular social and cultural locations.

To approach the Bible contextually means that we (1) move beyond the private zones of existence and listen with sensitivity to the otherwise muted voices in church and society; (2) get in touch with our own and others' yearning for freedom from despair, isolation, bondage, oppression, and guilt; (3) listen to Scripture in and with the faith community, in memory of people who have gone before and in hope for those who come after; (4) get in touch with the conversations the church has carried on in its creeds, confessions, and other expressions of faith.

2. We can approach the Bible *historically*, without fixating on the past. This means we take seriously the particularity of God's actions through Israel and in Jesus Christ. We also take seriously the fact that the biblical writers were limited, fallible human beings. Fully human words, marked by human particularity and limitations, disclose the divine word to us.

This approach means, further, that we live by the conviction that God's history is not yet actualized. We are promised its future fulfillment under the guidance of the Spirit. Hence, we are to read the Story as an unfolding story, with an eye to its extension. We can ask each other not only "What past does this recall?" but also "What future does it open up?" Together we must ask, "What claims does this make on the uses and directions of myself and my talents (*viz.*, vocation)? What claims are laid on my particular congregation? What is our specific calling as the faith community in this time, at this place?"

3. We can read the Scripture *theocentrically*. For Barth, narrative is an authoritative aspect of Scripture precisely

because it renders the identity description of a single agent, namely God. Through two sets of patterns—the history of Israel and the Story of Jesus—the canon reveals the character of the selfsame agent, God in Jesus Christ.[32] This rendering of one selfsame agent constitutes the unity of the Bible, Old and New Testament alike. "The history of Israel enacts in a collective way the same intentions as are re-enacted in a concretely personal way in the history of Jesus."[33] On a practical level, this means we must preach and teach the Old and New Testaments alike!

Whatever else was happening to characters in the biblical Story, one thing is certain. They were always undergoing God's action upon them. God is at the center of this Story. To participate, we must be willing to undergo a continuous revolution of how we understand and relate to God.

4. We can read Scripture with a *hermeneutic of suspicion*. That is, we can hold before ourselves the fact that Scriptures have been used to justify slavery, sexual oppression, nationalism, and the like. When we authentically engage with the Scriptures, we expose ourselves to an ongoing critique of these various ideologies.

Feminist biblical scholars, for example, are facing head-on the pervasive sexism within biblical materials. The Bible is unabashedly a male book, written by men in their language and thought forms, reflecting the male-centered biblical cultural milieu. The hermeneutics of suspicion proceeds by uncovering as much as possible the oppressive, patriarchal elements within the Scriptures.[34] It demonstrates the intrinsic connection of patriarchy to the whole social system of graded subjugations and oppressions related to race, class, and gender. This hermeneutic *does*, however, affirm the liberating, inspiring power of the Bible. It assumes that women and men alike should submit themselves to the authority of God's Word that the Bible mediates.

5. In order to hear God's liberating Word, we can read the

scriptures with a *hermeneutic of remembrance.* Feminist theologians remind us that we simply cannot deny those cases where the religious vision and self-understanding revealed in the text is clearly mistaken, is sinful or self-deceiving. We must remember with no whitewashing the struggles and suffering of our foremothers whose stories are hidden behind the texts. When read in this way, the Story establishes in us a "dangerous and subversive memory" and draws us into solidarity with victims of bondage, past and present.

6. Finally, we can read the Scriptures with a *hermeneutic of participation in the Story.* As Migliore suggests, "If both the Old and New Testaments have their center in narratives of God's liberating activity, these narratives were told and retold in Israel and in the early church because they were not yet finished."[35] God's history of liberation and reconciliation is open and ongoing! God is writing us into the Story!

7

Christian Spiritual Formation

—such a price
The God's exact for song:
To become what we sing.[1]

Christian spiritual formation is a matter of becoming the song that we sing, the Story we tell. We ourselves are to become the living texts of Christianity. Christianity is a message intended not to describe the world but to transform its hearers so that they may see for themselves the true character of reality. Its very intent is formation, not information. Our task is to let the Story so live through us that we are transformed to be as the Story is.[2]

Becoming Christian, then, involves a real change in the believer. In terms of traditional theology, the process of change is understood as sanctification or conversion. Today, changes in human personality commonly are called developmental stages and transitions. This chapter argues that sanctification is not best described by recourse to structural-developmental stages of faith, as is popular today. Sanctification is best understood, rather, through discourse about character. Sanctification is the lifelong process of formation and transformation of Christian character.

Rather than a matter of predictable, irreversible stages, formation of character is like an unfolding drama, with unpredictable twists and turns in the plot. There are fits and starts, sudden shifts and surprises, as well as imperceptible growth. Christian character is shaped as believers learn, through the guidance of the faith community, to orient their entire existence according to God's redeeming work in Jesus Christ. Formation, understood in this light, is the guiding image for Christian educational ministry.

This is not to say that formation of Christian character is in and of itself the direct goal of Christian education. Formation of Christian character is actually an *indirect* matter. We are not to get up each morning and wonder if we are more formed than the day before. Our call is not to fixate on self-formation but to follow Christ and learn to live his Story as our own.

A key thesis is that spiritual formation is not a thing apart from but rather the core dynamic in becoming Christian. Karl Barth wrote about Christian education as *Bildung* ("formation"), meaning an ongoing shaping process.[3] Whereas in contemporary literature formation often refers to a program of training in prayer and meditation (which, of course, are not beside the point!), Barth insisted that formation does not refer to certain practices or programs. Rather, it refers to the lifelong process of being conformed to the *imago Dei* as revealed in Jesus Christ. Formation is seen biblically as being changed into the truly human form revealed in Jesus Christ. The root *morphe* means "true as opposed to false form." We are not to be like Adam and try to become as God. We are to be like Christ, who became fully human. Christ brings the truly human in us to light. Our formation is contained, prefigured, and fulfilled in our participation in his Story. God in Christ is the true educator who calls forth and sustains formation over against our human efforts. As Barth says, "Grace makes good what we do not make good."[4]

In *Contemporary Approaches to Christian Education,* edited by Jack Seymour and Donald Miller,[5] various authors present five alternative ways to think about Christian education, through the images of faith development, interpretation, faith community (socialization-enculturation), religious instruction, and liberation. This book proposes *formation* as a decisive image through which to understand Christian education. One can detect in Seymour and Miller's survey the nascent appearance of spiritual formation as a guiding image, though its distinctiveness disappears into developmentalism, on the one hand, and the faith community model, on the other.

THE DOMINANCE OF DEVELOPMENTALISM

Do not be conformed to this world but be transformed by the renewal of your mind, that you may prove what is the will of God, what is good and acceptable and perfect. (Rom. 12:2)

Because we know that following Christ and living his Story requires us to become what we were not, Christian educators seek to understand what the change entails, how it happens, and how the faith community can best sponsor the process. Paul and other biblical writers expected believers to obtain Christian maturity. Over the course of centuries, the church has developed various conceptions of the mature Christian life. Throughout most of Christian history, spiritual theology provided the dominant approach.

Change and transformation in the religious life are understood in the twentieth century, however, mainly through a psychological rather than a theological perspective. For several decades religious education has, in my estimation, basked too much in the euphoria of developmental psychology. Consequently, psychology tends to drown out other voices, especially that of theology, in conversation about human change and growth, as Christianity understands it.

PSYCHOLOGICAL APPROACHES TO HUMAN CHANGE AND GROWTH

Foundational to theory and practice in Christian education today are developmental theories rooted in psycho-dynamic thought (Freud, Jung, Erikson) and in structural-developmental theory (Piaget, Kohlberg, Fowler). Equally influential in the growing field of spiritual psychology are the self-actualization (Maslow, Jung) and transpersonal (Ken Wilbur) schools of thought.

Freud focused on the dynamics of the *libido,* the quantum of generalized sexual and psychic energy available to individuals at birth. The psychosexual development of the child is mapped in stages according to how libidinal energy is focalized and transformed throughout the life-span. Freud also studied the ways in which energy is used by three differentiated systems of the personality: the *id,* the *ego,* and the *superego.* Mainly studying their conflicts and aberrations, Freud tended to view the human being as little more than a complex system of tension-reducing mechanisms.

Because he observed that Freud studied only the sick half of society, Abraham Maslow set about to study the healthy half. Rejecting Freud's notion that humans are essentially tension reducing, Maslow viewed persons as creative, open to change and growth, and prone to transcendent experiences he called *peak experiences.* For Maslow, human personality can best be understood as a lifelong process of self-actualization (i.e., *eudaimonism*).

Jung's work is a more complex variation of themes in Maslow. Though used less widely by religious educators, his work is popular among theorists in the area of spiritual psychology (cf. Morton Kelsey). His concept of *individuation* is important. Individuation is the lifelong process of discovering, refining, and integrating all the polar opposites that constitute the human personality.

Probably the most widely influential divergence from traditional psychodynamic theory is the ego psychology of Erik Erikson. Erikson shifted his focus from the dynamics of the libido to the lifelong development of the ego. For Erikson, the ego develops through eight stages during the human life cycle. Religious educators have looked to these stages as a way to understand the human journey to wholeness and maturity. At each new stage, the ego must interrelate biological, psychological, social, and cultural factors to achieve a stabilized sense of self. Each succeeding stage is predicated by a developmental crisis, out of which the person must synthesize both positive and negative elements.

The structural-developmental school of thought employs the notion of stage in a stricter fashion than do the life cycle theories. Structural-developmentalism focuses on formal, genetically given structures, sometimes referred to as computer-like programs or laws innate in the human mind, which develop more or less according to a biological time clock. A structure structures. It is a dynamic, patterned way of organizing one's experience and one's sense of reality. As such, each structure (stage) is governed by its own internal logic. New stages represent increasingly complex and differentiated ways of structuring the world.

Jean Piaget, the Swiss psychologist (and genetic episte-mologist), founded the structural-developmental school of thought, identifying the sequential stages of cognitive, intellectual development. Building on Piaget's work, Lawrence Kohlberg argued that there are six generalized, sequential patterns by which persons resolve moral dilemmas and develop morally.

Structural-developmental theorists claim that the structures are (1) universal, that is, applicable to every single human being at any given time and place; (2) sequential, following a set pattern; (3) invariant, building on one another in such a way that none can be skipped; (4) hierarchical, ascending in their degree of complexity; (5) formal, that is, free of any particular content.

In this decade, the religious education enterprise has been captivated by faith development theory, originally set forth by James Fowler.[6] Based upon structural-developmentalism, the theory construes faith as developing from one predictable, irreversible stage to the next. Fowler defines faith as basically a lawful quest for meaning. It has to do with how all individuals construct or structure a sense of a meaningful ultimate environment. As a general structure of human awareness, and an activity of making meaning, faith is universal, whether or not one is a religious believer. All persons have an operative faith, Fowler claims.

Faith, according to the theory, is structured by six distinctive stages over a lifetime. Each faith stage, constituted by seven formal aspects, operates according to its own internal logic. Faith progresses toward a greater degree of internal complexity and cognitive refinement of the seven formal dimensions. The six faith stages are intuitive-projective, mythic-literal, synthetic-conventional, individuative-reflective, conjunctive, and universalizing. Through these stages faith undergoes continuous development throughout the life cycle, following an invariant and hierarchical progression.

EGO, SELF, CHRISTIAN SELF

Common to each of the developmental theories described above is that they identify the human ego as the locus of a person's change, growth, and development. Though the ego is part of the given substratum with which we must contend for the rest of our lives, it is neither the final determinant of, nor the best way to talk about, Christian self-identity. The ego *tries* to be the center of personality, but for the Christian it cannot, even though developmental theory traces and underwrites this position.

Because Fowler deals with faith as the basic function of the ego, he does not deal adequately with the *total self* as it acquires its basic identity (and content) under the impact of the Christian Story. Yet, this is the phenomenon that matters most to Christian formation.

Moreover, though Fowler acknowledges the importance of affections, he tends to focus only on the linear development of the *rational* core of human beings. The fiduciary (trust) and virtue dimensions of faith—so central to the biblical portrait of it—do not appear in the seven formal aspects of each faith stage. The ego functions Fowler does examine are all functions of human cognition. Mary Ford-Grabowksy convincingly argues that there are cultural and male-oriented biases that cause Fowler to narrowly focus on the ego, neglecting the concept of self; to focus on cognition, neglecting religious affections; to focus on positive aspects of development, neglecting sin and deception as stumbling blocks to faith.[7]

Ego psychology, when taken alone, shrinks our understanding of the human person. The ego is only one among other psychological systems, and so our understanding of Christian formation must be situated in a more comprehensive way of talking about persons. There are various ways to talk about the phenomenon larger than the conscious ego. One of those ways is through the language of the self.

The self is a more socially determined construct than is the ego, though the capacity for self-transcendence and self-agency is influenced by ego development. The self is awakened in the course of human development through interaction with other selves in community, and exists as a self only in such relationships. According to the American tradition of social psychology (cf. William James and George Herbert Mead), through socialization we each internalize a "social self" based on the attitudes and responses of significant respected others toward us. We judge, praise, blame, approve, disapprove, like, or dislike ourselves based upon internal scenarios of what significant others might say.

Yet as a self we can learn to accept, reject, and select socially imposed experience. Maturity, in fact, requires us to increasingly assume personal responsibility for sifting and sorting culturally imposed self-definitions. Self-agency means that we have the capacity to choose (to some degree) an unconditioned response to life. We can decide to change much about ourselves.

As Christian selves, however, we are called to a maturity and transformation beyond our own ability to change ourselves. To live "in the Spirit" complicates rather than simplifies life. As Christians we are commanded not only to love our neighbors but also to care for even our enemies, and to provide hospitality to strangers. We are summoned, further, to trust God in the face of the tragic, to refuse to despair when life gets desperate, to hope when there's nothing hopeful in sight, to forgive when retaliation would feel much better, to be at peace in the face of death, to let go of securing ourselves through unending achievement and acquisition.

This requires a radical new form of existence that, as we all know, is difficult to squeeze out from our own wills. But to live "in the Spirit" is to receive as a gift that which we cannot obtain by the direct efforts of our own will. Through the Spirit, we receive time and again the grace that transforms the shortcomings of our own will and the self-centered, relentless demands of our ego. And all this is at God's gracious initiative. It is not our own doing.

Only when grounded and centered in the very Power by which it exists at all, therefore, may the self transcend even itself. This new, transcendent self is self as spirit, the spiritual self or the "free pneumatic self."[8] Christian spiritual formation, put in these terms, is our gradual transformation from a biological and socially mediated self into the more remarkable phenomenon of self as spirit. Hence, we must speak of spiritual development rather than ego development to signal the transcendence that bridges the ego and the self.[9] Because this transcendence is dynamic not static, at any time we can relapse and fall back into determinism. It is misleading, consequently, to think of spiritual formation in term of invariant, hierarchical, or lawful progression.

CHRISTIAN CHARACTER AND CHRISTIAN EDUCATION

The Eclipse of Character

The notion of spiritual self points us beyond the ego and the social self to the reality of the Christian self or Christian character. The sacralization of stage theory has led to the eclipse of character and correspondingly appropriate virtues. We have given scant attention to the shape of character required for, and called forth by, participating in the creative and redemptive work of God.

Formation of Christian character simply does not share the scientific predictability of stage sequence. The inbreaking work of the Spirit is not so easily scheduled, nor the human soul so easily mapped! Christians are made, not born (Tertullian). But they do not simply "develop." Christian formation is much messier than that, full as it is of detours and deserts, wanderings and awakenings.

The Christian journey is not best mapped by structurally invariant stages but rather by the master stories and sentiments by which we attempt, and sometimes fail, to orient our lives. We acquire a certain character not due to particular processes or underlying structures but due to the particular content that qualifies us. Christian formation pivots on our stories of loyalty and betrayal, trust and suspicion, of the One who is always faithful to us. Character is fundamentally an unfolding narrative, shaped in the drama, the tensions and conflicts of attempting to negotiate the Christian Story as our own story.

The Elements of Character

Character refers to the most basic determination of who we are as persons. It is the language of self-identity. Nothing is more basic about us than our character. Character is the content of who "I" am and who "you" are as unique individuals. It would be impossible to present a comprehensive definition of character here. Rather, I shall simply list eight areas of exploration that the concept of character, Christianly understood, opens up for us.[10]

1. *Character refers to a whole, created person, including our unconscious.* Whereas Greek philosophy taught a body-soul dualism, biblical writers portray the human being as a created, whole person, animated by the breath or Spirit of God (Gen. 2:7). The apostle Paul did not define persons in dualistic terms, though he often used polar contrasts, such as old nature/new nature (Eph. 4:22-24; Col. 3:9-10); flesh/spirit (Rom. 8:10); old self/new self (Rom. 6:6); outer nature/inner nature (II Cor. 4:16); and spiritual person/unspiritual person (I Cor. 2:14-15). He also referred to the "inmost self" (Rom. 7:22) and "inner man" (Eph. 3:16).

Paul did not intend a "real self" (nonmaterial substance hidden within) over against fallen flesh or corporeal existence. When Paul spoke of those who live "according to the flesh," he was definitely not denigrating the human body, sexuality, or material existence. He was speaking about that portion of humanity, that portion of ourselves, that lives on as if God does not exist.

The fundamental contrast for Paul is between life lived wholly under the pervasive influence of God's Spirit, and life that utterly refuses and resists the Spirit. "Inmost self" and "inner nature" do not refer to some nonmaterial essence hidden behind our character. They are ways to talk about our *true* nature as creatures of God. For Paul they serve as references to Christian character, that is, our whole human existence as qualified and determined by the creative, mysterious breath of God's Spirit.

2. *Character refers to the fundamental way we intend the world.* Christian character is forged in the vital dialectic between our intentions and our actions. To be a Christian means learning to see or intend the world in a particular way, and thus to become as we see.[11] This is closely linked to the biblical notion of discernment (cf. I Cor. 2:14). When we turn to Christ, we are invited by him to see the world in terms of the inbreaking Realm of God, and to reshape ourselves and the world accordingly. Christian character has to do, therefore, with the capacity to truthfully see ourselves, to let go of self-deception, and to see and join the world as it really is. We do not see just by looking but by having our attention trained through spiritual discipline undertaken in community.

Christian character, in terms of everyday reality, has to do with the intent to see our co-workers and colleagues and the strangers we meet as fellow creatures and fellow sufferers rather than fundamentally as threats to our security. It means we come to see and admit our need to love and to be loved just as we are. It means the capacity to confess how sometimes we ignore, ridicule, exploit, or marginalize people who are different. It means we stop trying to acquire, buy, control, or consume all that we need and learn, rather, to receive it from our Creator and from one another.

3. *Character involves the shape of our interiority, our inmost*

dispositions, affections, and attitudes. Scripture reveals a God concerned with the condition of the human heart, the biblical metaphor for character. The biblical insight is that who we *are* is as important as, and inseparable from, what we do, believe, or say. God desires that the whole person be formed in love (Deut. 6:5).

This means that a rich interiority is important to Christian character, though spirituality is more than interiority. Though it often demands instantaneous self-revelation, much modern spirituality encourages privatism. There is such a thing as genuine privacy, but we have reduced it to privatism. Privatism excludes; interiority includes. Privatism means keeping everything to oneself; interiority means preparing oneself to share. Privatism focuses only on the self; interiority entails an inward relationship with outside objects. Privatism guards space; interiority grows a garden of graciousness.

Modern self-help people suffer impoverishment of interiority because they think it means only to grovel in the goo of gut level feelings. Interiority is, however, the creation of a sacred inner space. It is where we may be playful and hopeful in our imagination; where we carry on imaginative dress rehearsals for genuine public living, where we sustain a rich inner dialogue of possibilities, where we recollect and repose in silence and solitude, where we begin to translate thought into speech and action, where we tend the fire of hospitality for strangers.

4. *Character involves what we do with all the givens in our lives.* Character means that we can become more than what is genetically, developmentally, and environmentally given to us. Character is what we do with the range of choices we *do* have, since there is so much givenness and so much that simply happens to us. No matter the weight of what perhaps tragically happens to us, we are still answerable for who we become. We can embrace, interpret, and fit into a meaningful

story all the givens of life: our physical appearance, our temperament, our psychological flaws, our social class, our cultural experience, our early upbringing, our suffering, and our sickness.

5. *Character is a gift of community.* Character is not something that we ourselves alone create. It is a gift of those who bring us up, and of those who continue to help nourish our Christian existence. As we mature, however, we assume increasing responsibility for the shape of our character. But originally it is the gift of community. Since character formation does not begin *de novo,* that is, from scratch, our calling is to build upon what has been given to us.

6. *Character is an ongoing, lifelong project.* Christian formation is never a fully accomplished fact or a static possession. We cannot acquire a certain character and then leave it unattended and uncultivated. Daily we make the decision to live by certain convictions rather than others. The character we have tomorrow depends fundamentally on what we decide to do with ourselves today. Our self-transcendence is constantly at stake. We are vulnerable, insecure, self-deceptive, and easily manipulated by cultural dictates rather than determined by Christian Story. Though we do have inconsistencies, Christian character means at least that we are committed to bringing every element of ourselves, everything we believe, feel, do, or do not do, into relation with our primary loyalty to God's Realm.[12] The shaping of our orientation to God's Realm is never finished once and for all.

7. *Character is the locus of sanctification.* To be determined by God's Realm, in terms of traditional theology, is to undergo sanctification. Sanctification refers to the actual formation of Christian character.[13] It is the result of ongoing conformity to the Story of God's work to make and keep human life human. Sanctification does not imply that we will or even should try to achieve "the sixth stage." It does mean that we must be caught up into a never-ending process of

learning how, more appropriately, more wholeheartedly, more deliberately, to participate in God's redemptive work in the world. To be sanctified is to deepen, to clarify, to intensify our overall participation with the church in the Realm of God. To this there is no final stage.

The grammar or logic of this growth cuts across a different plane than the hierarchy of structural stages. If anything, this dynamic of change can be pictured as a spiral that dips up and down, that expands and contracts as we are faithful and unfaithful, loyal and disloyal, to the One in whom "there is no shadow of turning." This will be a lifelong process of centering, de-centering, and recentering ourselves, with others, in Christ.

8. *Christian character requires Christian education.* To acquire Christian character means we must be trained by the faith community to see and to take part in the world rendered by the Christian Story. Formation, as an ongoing process, thus requires a community of intentionally lived faith, disciplined in its spiritual life. Such a community will be very deliberate in Christian initiation, training new believers from the outset in prayer and meditation, searching the Scriptures, confession and repentance, praise and proclamation, works of mercy and justice.

Because it does require such cultivation, Christian formation runs the risk of being reduced to a special program offered by the church, dissected from a whole way of being in the world.[14] Earlier in this century, for example, Ernest M. Ligon, head of the Character Research Project at Union College in Schenectady, New York, erred in trying to make character formation into a science, replete with trait taxonomies. There is, however, no preset, fixed pattern for Christian character, though certainly there are spiritual exemplars whose lives we can commend.

Christian character must arise as a wholehearted way of following a Person and living creatively within the Realm he teaches us to see. The final shape of Christian character will be as varied and unique as the individuals who have come by it. There are textbook versions of normative "ages and stages." There is no textbook prescription for Christian character. Formation is not a highly distilled grab-bag of virtues. It is a matter of being loyal to a Person and conformed to the Story that helps us negotiate the unending variety of conflicting loyalties that confront us throughout a lifetime.[15]

As we attempt in Christian education to help one another "rekindle the gift of God that is within" (II Tim. 1:16), something important will happen, and it will have to do with character.

FORMATION AND TRANSFORMATION

The formation of Christian character implies *transformations* of character. In being conformed to Christ, we will be led through radical breaks, deaths, and rebirths, painful wrenchings and surprising breakthroughs. Formation is a way to talk about the everyday continuities of becoming Christian, whereas transformation is more of a way to talk about the discontinuities, or the "big events." Formation and transformation, processes and events, are woven together in the lifelong process of conversion, of becoming Christian, of shaping Christian character.

James Loder is the Christian education theorist most interested in the theme of Christian transformation. In his book *The Transforming Moment*, Loder explores the dynamics or the logic of faith transformation.[16] Rather than focusing on a series of stages, however, he gives attention to convictional experiences, or transforming moments, through which the believer's entire existence is radically changed.

Through Loder's work we can see that it is not necessarily the predictable series of stages and transitions that most profoundly shape us. Rather, it is what happens to us within the "unscheduled crises," when we receive the grim phone call in the night that undoes our taken-for-granted sense of reality. In the face of the tragic, we find ourselves grounded even as we are yanked into the dark abyss. Within the logic of transformation, the latter stages are less the product and more the transformer of previous stages of development. Transforming moments *refigure* our past and *prefigure* our future!

Loder underscores H. R. Niebuhr's contention that the revelatory moment is not the mere development of faith already held. It is, rather, the creation of faith itself, or else faith's radical and permanent reconstruction. It is radical, Niebuhr says, because it makes a new beginning and puts an end to old development, and it is permanent because it never comes to an end in time.[17] Faith, therefore, is indeed central to Christian character, as Fowler would have it, but it is not merely an ongoing and general structure of human awareness. Within an explicitly biblical perspective, it is difficult to see how faith can be construed as a natural organ of human development. There is an event quality to faith, as it must authenticate itself time and again. Faith has to do with actually *being faithful*—to God!—in this or that situation. And biblically speaking, it is always a participation in God's power, not our own capacities.

SUMMARY

Perhaps out of respect for pluralism, Christian religious educators seem to have shied away from contributing a partisan, explicitly biblical or theological understanding of human transformation. Because contemporary psychology purports to be an empirically verifiable science, biblical metaphors for transformation may seem imprecise, parochial, and primitive. Yet in the human-divine encounter with the primal narrative from which these metaphors emerge, we experience time and again an impact that is particular, concrete, radical, and transformative.[18]

Difficult as it is to achieve, we need to work toward a truly *interdisciplinary* understanding of Christian change and transformation. We seem to over-rely on social science. In its approach to character and virtue, theological ethics has tended to be overlooked as an important resource to Christian education and to theological anthropology. In the field of psychology, moreover, a more promising conversation partner than cognitive structuralism is object relations theory. This theory emphasizes the interpersonal side of psychodynamic thought, focusing on how the human person is formed through the media of interpersonal relationships and relatedness to meaningful objects in the environment.

The structural-developmental theory of faith, however, is by no means to be dismissed as irrelevant. We simply need to rethink our use of it. Here are some things I suggest we keep in mind.

1. Developmental theories tend to suggest their own built-in norms and rules for use. They bear psychic pressure on us to do this rather than that in our ministry. No theory is value-free, and so we must pay attention not only to what we do with the theory but also to what it does to us.

2. We must not be seduced into using faith theory for purposes of *intervention* in ministry, that is, to try to prompt persons to move from one stage to the next. The pernicious implication here is that persons in earlier stages are somehow incomplete or immature beings and will remain so until they progress through all six stages. If we turn persons into "projects," we subtly create I-It rather than I-Thou relationships with them. We need an approach that subjectifies rather than objectifies persons.

3. Cognitive complexity does not exhaust the biblical understanding of faith. A "higher" stage may open up new cognitive possibilities but it does not guarantee our participation in God's work, nor determine the depth, insight, or faithfulness of it. At any so-called stage we may

obtain the life commended by the gospel (Mark 12:30) or miss it altogether.

4. Faith development theory is pressed by some leaders into an overall organizing model for ministry. It cannot, however, bear this burden. Faith development theory is best seen as but one *research tool*, among others, in helping us calibrate resources and environments for teaching/learning.

5. Faith development theory *does* measure some developmental phenomena, to be sure, but it does not measure the progress of faith, biblically understood. The theory concentrates too narrowly on ego psychology to do that. There are several possibilities as to what it does measure: (1) increasing competency of the ego in structuring meaning; (2) ascending cognitive complexity in processing information; (3) shifting styles of self-world understanding. If the theory traces something that is truly linear and hierarchical, then most likely it is the developing (cognitive) capacity of persons to form fully reflective and critical understandings of faith (*if* they have any) or, as far as that goes, anything else.

The most important consideration is our use of faith development theory. Lest we be seduced by a sinful "creeping intellectual elitism" (Hauerwas), we must stretch ourselves toward obtaining purity of heart and integrity of character rather than a "higher" cognitive structure!

8

Church: An Ecology of Spiritual Care and Formation

By its very nature, the church is an ecology of spiritual care and guidance. It is the decisive context for Christian spiritual formation. The church offers tacit as well as direct spiritual care and direction as it catches people up into what it is and does. Through its witness and service, through dramatizing the Story in liturgy and paraliturgy, through preaching and teaching and singing and praying, the church gives practical spiritual guidance.

Spiritual guidance includes training persons in the skills and disciplines (means of grace) ingredient to living the Christian Story. These are fundamentally the means by which the church itself participates in and initiates persons into the Realm of God. The focal setting for spiritual guidance is worship, as we gather to do our liturgy. We initiate, form, and guide Christians through our common prayer and private prayer, through our giving, receiving, rejoicing, confessing, adopting, naming, instructing, washing, anointing, blessing. These are gestures necessary to our formation that the church does *to* us, *for* us, *with* us.

Spiritual guidance and care in the congregation must be ongoing and consistent, woven into the fabric of all that happens rather than presented on sporadic occasions as a new program. Many elements of spiritual guidance and care can be initiated and ritualized by pastors and Christian educators who themselves are responsible for breaking the silence about spirituality.[1]

The representation below helps us to situate our understanding of the dimensions of spiritual guidance in the congregation (fig. 8.1).[2] The remainder of this chapter will explicate each of these dimensions.

ENVIRONMENT OF GRACE

"For by grace you have been saved through faith; and this is not your own doing, it is the gift of God" (Eph. 2:8). Within the church are many gifts that help us learn to participate in the mystery of our salvation. The ministry of spiritual guidance begins in the theological conviction that we have been given a share in God's creative and redemptive activity and that we must be initiated by the faith community in order for us to see and participate in it.

"See to it that no one fail to obtain the grace of God" (Heb. 12:15). This charge for ministry and witness is given to the entire company of believers, not simply the clerics. We are to witness to the whole world that the fundamental context of life is the unbounded love and redemptive grace of God. To fulfill their vocational call, every Christian already has a spiritual guide in the presence of God's Spirit (I John 5:7-10). Our task is not to usurp or take over for God, but to help each other pay attention to the motions of grace and the promptings of the Spirit.

The ultimate context of spiritual formation and guidance, thus, is the environment of grace. *Spiritus creator* is already present, not imported by us, as a creating, converting, guiding

Figure 8.1.

The Church: An Ecology of
Spiritual Care and Christian Formation

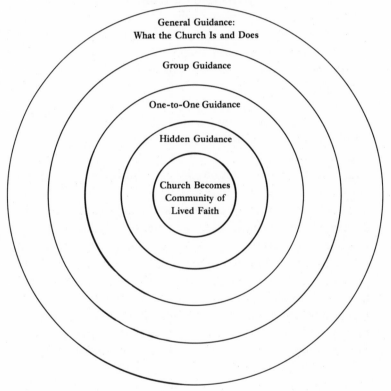

Initiation into the Realm of God

General Guidance:
What the Church Is and Does

Group Guidance

One-to-One Guidance

Hidden Guidance

Church Becomes
Community of
Lived Faith

presence. Pastors, educators, and teachers are qualified by this transcendent context of ministry: "So neither he who plants nor he who waters is anything, but only God who gives the growth" (I Cor. 3:7).

GENERAL GUIDANCE: WHAT THE CHURCH IS AND DOES

Some people want to make the church beside the point in Christian faith, yet Paul and other biblical writers insist that we cannot do this! Ephesians insists that it is the church itself that is being built into God's redemptive activity in the world. Through the church and owing to the church, we share in that work.

Participation in God's *oikoumene*, God's divine activity in all creation, is taught and learned in the local congregation. Participation begins simply and moves to the complex as we become more and more involved in the manifold relationships of Christian community. Self-involvement in the church's life, broadly understood, is the key to learning.

Seen in this light, the curriculum of Christian education is conceived broadly as the planned, intentional environment of teaching and learning to participate. The curriculum is what the people take home with them from their experience in the congregation, says Howard Grimes. Its content, he suggests, includes "the total meaning of all that happens: words, relationships, deeds, actions, participation."[3] Powerful modes of Christian formation include the informal and often unconscious appropriation of the beliefs, affections, and actions of what a Christian is and what a Christian does.

The congregation is where we encounter people who know something already of negotiating a Christian life. Our ability to pray, to do justice, and to love mercy develops only if we so keep company that a "participant" is incorporated into our own consciousness.

Attending to the lives of official and ordinary saints within the extended community is a vital means of spiritual formation. Training in Christianity fundamentally is training in following a person. Those who have learned to follow provide us with paradigms of growth and maturity in the Christian life. We learn what it means to follow Christ mainly through watching how other believers from many times, places, and circumstances have followed.

We are compelled by the autobiographical and biographical accounts, for instance, of Edith Stein as she risked her life teaching in Nazi Germany and helping fellow sufferers at Auschwitz; Catherine as she cared for lepers and plague victims in Siena; Saint Augustine in his conversion in the garden; Dame Julian as she offered spiritual counsel at Norwich; Simone Weil as she grew up identifying with the underprivileged, the common laborers, and Nazi victims in France; Martin Luther King as he led the nonviolent civil rights movement; Mother Teresa working with the sick and starving in the streets of Calcutta; Dag Hammarskjold in his governmental role; Dorothy Day as she worked with the urban homeless and hungry, founding the Catholic Worker Movement.

Our task is to discern and to direct attention to individuals whose lives provide a compelling witness to the Judeo-Christian Story. Yet our cloud of witnesses includes not only the lives of spiritual exemplars but also testimony found in councils, creeds, confessions, catechisms, doctrines, and rituals. In the church we affirm ecclesial formulations and spiritual writings as sources of wisdom, authority, and encouragement. "For whatever was written in former days was written for our instruction, that . . . encouragement of the scriptures we might have hope" (Rom. 15:4).

Investigation and inquiry into our tradition, therefore, is an important aspect of initiation into the Story. Such inquiry is one bridge between the teaching office of the church and its office of spiritual direction. The ecclesial memory of many Christians today is far too short! Informal processes of socialization, powerful as they are, cannot replace structured settings in which we investigate together the church's historical as well as its present experience in the world.

GROUP GUIDANCE

Two are better than one, because they have a good reward. . . .For if they fall, one will lift up his fellow; but woe to him who is alone when he falls and has not another to lift him up. (Eccles. 4:9-10)

Group settings have always been one of the most vital contexts for spiritual formation and guidance. Jesus spent most of his time with groups. Settings for group guidance range from early monastic communities to John Wesley's class meetings to contemporary intentional communities, such as Iona and Taizé. Present day group settings include faith sharing groups, family clusters, Sunday School classes, guided retreat programs such as Walk to Emmaus and Cursillo, retreat houses, prayer groups, house church meetings, seminary formation groups, inquiry classes, baptismal catechesis groups, as well as informal networks of support.

Groups offer settings wherein a tremendous measure of spiritual guidance happens in quite ordinary ways. They provide a direct, intense, interpersonal environment where we learn from watching how others negotiate the Christian life. Within small groups we gain informal, "around the coffee pot" spiritual support, as well as a formal structure for learning. Groups offer a lifelong context of companionship in the Christian life. They seem to function best when comprised of no more than eight to twelve persons who gather out of a covenantal understanding of their relationship together. The perennial issues for group members include personal accountability, privacy, freedom, plurality of Christian lifestyles, confidentiality, and trust.

Whether groups meet in retreat settings, in homes, or elsewhere, the key elements to be balanced are (1) practicing together the spiritual disciplines, (2) learning to make God's Realm concrete in our daily lives (praxis), (3) training in the various lay ministries of the church and in realizing Christian vocation, and (4) investigating the length and breadth of the Christian Story.

Spiritual care in groups requires that we create space for persons to hear their own hearts, space for persons to speak, and space for others to listen. This space is born of freedom, respect, trust, and intimacy. Only in such an environment can we attune ourselves to the personal presence of one another. Such an environment respects privacy (not privatism!) as an appropriate, important aspect of spiritual intimacy. Only pseudointimacy requires instantaneous, intrusive, all-encompassing self-disclosure of one's inmost feelings (and the emphasis is always on feeling, not on complex thoughts!)

Authentic intimacy is transformational in character, partly because we discover through it that reality "out there" is not indifferent to our presence. Personhood emerges and is sustained only when we feel we are noticed, cherished, valued, and loved as unique individuals. Christian education must be founded on the personal, interrelational structure of reality. This means, as well, that if we are to love as God loves, we must not be indifferent to the presence of strangers.

When face-to-face groups flourish, there exists a greater possibility for creativity in Christian care. Christian love makes ordinary people extraordinary in their responses to each other. Love needs no professional experts. Consider the friends of the paralytic and the creativity prompted by their compassion:

And when [Jesus] returned to Capernaum after some days, it was reported that he was at home. And many were gathered together, so that there was no longer room for them, not even about the door; and he was preaching the word to them. And they came, bringing to him a paralytic carried by four men. And when they could not get near him because of the crowd, they removed the roof above him; and when they had made an opening, they let down the pallet on which the paralytic lay. And when Jesus saw their faith, he said to the paralytic, "My son, your sins are forgiven." (Mark 2:1-5)

What marvelous imagery! When the friends of the paralytic could not as much as get near the front door, they decided to poke a hole in the roof of Jesus' home. Imagine yourself doing that! The covenant community, our new family, mediates God's healing presence when we lose sight of it. Within community, especially in the intimacy of small groups, we are loved into being who we are. Not only are we loved, but we are also confronted, challenged, carried, anointed, blessed.

The creativity of Christian community pictured in Mark 2 stands as a corrective to the privatistic spirituality that we often find in our churches. Compare Mark 2 with the isolation we do find in the story of John 5. In presenting an assignment for a seminary Christian education course, a particular group of students invited the rest of the class to join in a role play. It was the story of Jesus healing the man by the pool of Bethzatha (John 5:2-9). As we gathered on the floor by the pool, we were to assume a posture as one of the "multitude of invalids, blind, lame, paralyzed." One of our class members was the sick man "who had been ill for thirty-eight years." I happened to be at the pool next to him.

Jesus came to Jerusalem, passing by the sheep gate and the pool. When he saw the man and knew he had been lying there for a long time, he said to him, "Do you want to be healed?" The sick man answered, "Sir, I have no [one] to put me into the pool when the water is troubled." I was dumbfounded! I was so familiar with the passage that I had become unable to hear anything new in it.

The words of the man who had been at the pool longer

than I had yet lived pierced through me. "I have no one . . ." His illness was not simply a private, physiological problem. It was a relational issue as well. ". . . while I am going another steps down before me." Perhaps the man *was* making up a lame excuse. Or perhaps there simply was no genuine community by the pool—just a collection of isolated individuals each awaiting their own shot at healing! The point is that illness—as well as health—implies our need for relationships in a community of spiritual care. Some of us at the pool could have chosen to be "wounded healers" (Nouwen). We could have carried the man into healing waters. We were all too self-preoccupied to think of it!

ONE-TO-ONE GUIDANCE

The ancient practice of individual spiritual direction is receiving renewed attention in the church today. Traditionally a dimension of the pastoral office in the Roman Catholic church, spiritual direction gradually evolved into a separate and distinct ministerial office. It also became a discipline of study, governed by its own specific body of knowledge called ascetical theology. The root word for ascetic is *asketikos*, from *askein*, which means "to discipline oneself in exercise and training." The apostle Paul used this image, for instance, in I Corinthians 9:24-27.

Spiritual direction gradually became more science than art. The Roman Catholic church, for instance, developed catalogues of principles and teachings on the important *regula* of spiritual perfection. Various types and divisions of sins were catalogued. Sins perceived as fatal to spiritual progress were catalogued as the deadly sins. Casuistry was the science of drawing upon the various catalogues in order to deal with cases of conscience and to resolve questions of moral conduct and decision making.

There were many excesses in this style of one-to-one

spiritual direction. It was riddled with authoritarian and patriarchal overtones. For this reason among others, to Protestant ears the phrase "spiritual director" has sounded too loaded with power and control. Unfortunately, rather than appropriating the riches of the classical spiritual tradition into a distinctively Protestant ethos, the Reformation housecleaning swept away virtually all notions of spiritual direction and formation.

Spiritual direction is fortunately being recovered by the Protestant church today. This is occurring on two fronts: as a normative dimension of the pastoral office and as a dimension of Christian ministry that all Christians may exercise by virtue of their baptism and Christian vocation.[4] We are beginning to provide models, training, and support for the mutual giving and receiving of spiritual care.

It is important today, however, not to define one-to-one spiritual guidance with a clerical bias. Profound spiritual care is given in quite ordinary ways as believers pour out their souls to each other, listening together for the promptings of God's Spirit.

The *diakonia* of spiritual care in the congregation depends upon a strong notion of the universal priesthood of all believers, to which pastors and educators belong *before* being set aside through ordination or consecration for special ministries![5] The responsibility for mutual spiritual care was implicit all along in the Protestant notion of the priesthood of all believers. It laid upon every believer a positive obligation to be a priest and spiritual guide for other Christian believers. How this was to be worked out in daily living, though, remained woefully underdeveloped.

Individual spiritual guidance may appear quite similar to psychotherapy and counseling, yet their bases are quite distinctive. Psychotherapy and counseling tend to be conducted on the basis of mutually recognized canons of theory and technique in semicontractual and formalized settings. They tend to address themselves to emotional crisis management and problem-solving skills. Spiritual guidance, however, is not basically crisis or problem centered, or related to emotional dysfunction.

Spiritual guidance concerns itself with the reality that in every Christian's life God's Spirit is distributing *charismata*, that is, gifts and graces for Christian vocation. Seen in this light, spiritual guidance is an art, an unfolding process rather than the application of specific techniques and procedures. Spiritual guidance aims to clarify Christian vocation, to quicken the image and likeness of God *(imago Dei)* within, to discern the motions of grace, and to discover resistances to it.

Spiritual guidance, at its most basic level, does not, therefore, require a specialized methodology or a specific technique. As we recover this ancient art, we must be careful neither to clericalize nor to professionalize it. Though intentionality and some human preparation is important, technique is not the primary ingredient. Bonhoeffer suggested that the simplicity of love takes precedence over therapeutic method. The work of spiritual guidance and care, he suggested, is essentially premethodical and prepsychological.[6] For him, spiritual guidance is the "path of familial assistance" toward hearing the proclamation of the good news and the promise of participation in it.[7] From the psychologist, the giver of spiritual direction can learn to listen, to observe, to evaluate, to be empathetic. Yet the real service of spiritual care is on a different level and of a different order.

In the terminology of the classic spiritual tradition, there is a "director" and a "directee" or "exercitant" who receives "direction." These terms can be misleading. A spiritual "director" is not so much a professional expert as a co-pilgrim with us on a common journey. More helpful images today include mentor, guide, companion, soul friend, spiritual friend, and faith sponsor. The benefit of one-to-one guidance lies in having an outside reference who can help us obtain clarity and self-insight.

HIDDEN GUIDANCE

The hidden dimension of guidance is closely associated with the concept of the hidden or implicit curriculum discussed by many educators. Elliot Eisner, for instance, suggests that all schools or institutions that serve a formative, educative function teach three curricula.[8]

Explicit Curriculum

The first or explicit level of curriculum is what we normally mean by curriculum, beginning first with the dated and undated materials ordered from a religious publishing house. Beyond this, explicit curriculum refers to other material and human resources that we utilize, the behaviors and beliefs we commend, the skills we teach, the activities and settings we provide, and all the ways we intentionally guide learners into the Story and give them spiritual care.

Hidden Curriculum

John Dewey suggested that "perhaps the greatest of all pedagogical fallacies is the notion that a person learns only the particular things that he [or she] is studying at the time."[9] Dewey was referring to what we teach and learn indirectly or tacitly. People take home with them much more than what we plan for them. There are many facets to the hidden, implicit curriculum in education and spiritual guidance.

The implicit curriculum includes the unspoken and the unconscious rules by which we socialize persons into the congregation. Through these processes we communicate a more or less hidden set of expectations that influence all dimensions of life together. Our education, for instance, may socialize persons into compliance and passivity, or into competitiveness and achievement addiction.

The implicit or hidden guidance impresses upon people what is and is not permissible to question or probe. It also suggests what is normative for the Christian life, regardless of what we teach explicitly. A congregation may talk about prayer, for instance, but never teach people *how* to pray and meditate. It may espouse the equality of all God's children yet disbar women from the pulpit and dissuade blacks from entering the sanctuary.

Hidden direction refers to what is praised and noted as worthy of attention, to all those things in which the congregation invests itself. Our life style leaves an impression of what is required absolutely and what is only optional or marginal to the Christian life. The implicit level of curriculum is that which is already *in* leaders and teachers, *in* structures, and *in* processes. Spiritual direction is tacit in a wide range of contexts, such as church retreats, youth and family camps, ongoing Bible study and prayer groups, training events, workshops, and pastoral conversations.

Implicit guidance includes that which is hidden within relationships, events, and settings. Further, it includes the stories, symbols, and values by which we have come to orient our lives but of which we are only dimly, if at all, aware.

The hidden spiritual guidance we give and receive in our faith communities shapes us in either a positive or a negative fashion. Most of us, unfortunately, receive much direction that dictates to us cultural rather than Christian values. We need to exercise the kind of spiritual discipline that can help us get in touch with these hidden directors so that we may choose for or against them. This surely is one meaning of "testing the spirits."

When Richard J. Foster suggests fasting, for instance, he points out that a fast from food is not the only fast that is spiritually helpful. It might help us to fast from the media, from the telephone, from the dictates of our consumer culture, from achievement addiction. As Foster points out, fasting reveals to us the things that really control us.[10] Fasting may help us get in touch with the negative hidden directors in our life.

Null Curriculum

There is a third level of curriculum in teaching and guidance: the null curriculum and the null guidance. This is obviously a paradox—a curriculum that does not exist! However, it is important for us to note what is being taught by what is *not* taught. The null curriculum refers to the fact that any given educational enterprise can choose *not* to initiate persons into some aspect of reality. This is not neutral!

The church has, throughout its history, rendered null and silent the experience of women. It has not particularly given voice to people of color, the poor and powerless. James Smart has documented "the strange silence of the Bible in the church."[11] Most Christians remain ignorant of how to read and resist the dominant culture. We still, without embarrassment, do not know how in the church to talk about our experience of our bodies and our sexuality. Mainline, liberal Christians are hesitant to share with each other their deepest spiritual yearnings and their hunger to draw nearer to God. The long, terrible silence about domestic violence and abuse is just beginning to crack open. Protestants are woefully out of touch with the riches of the classic spiritual tradition. Christians largely do not know the church's experience of itself and its circumstances throughout history, or across the globe today. We live in poverty of inclusive and feminine metaphors to talk about God's reality in our lives. These are all vivid examples of the null—silenced—curriculum in contemporary Christian education.

The null curriculum affects the values we adopt, the

perspectives we choose, the dispositions we develop, the character we form, and the community we become. The absence of a set of considerations biases what we are able to see. It diminishes us and our access to reality.

The two major components of the null curriculum include specific *content* as well as specific *processes* left out of consideration. Null curriculum reminds us of the power of language to form or deform. Language can effect, reveal, and disclose reality, or it can destroy, conceal, and suppress reality. The spoken word is powerful if not dangerous! This is why no words can come to us at times from Soweto in South Africa.

One important task of Christian education is to help the church become critically aware of what it teaches in its latent, implicit curriculum, as well as what it has silenced altogether in its historic witness, worship, and work.

SUMMARY

The church, especially the congregation, is a rich ecology of spiritual care. Ecology is a notion that underscores the organic, interrelated, multivalent levels of education and guidance we give and receive in all that we say and do in the church. In chapter 9 we shall further explore the intentional side of this ministry.

9

Christian Education for Formation

While formation takes place in quite ordinary and spontaneous ways, it cannot be left to chance. On the other hand, formation of character is not something that can be entirely planned. Much formation is indirect. What *can* be directly is deliberate, systematic, and intentional education in the church. When the church is significantly alive in its awareness and involvement in God's redemptive activity, the shaping of Christian character significantly takes root.

Formation as our educational intention reorients the way we define the nature and tasks of Christian education, and the things to which we pay educational attention in the congregation. How might concern for Christian spiritual formation alter our view of curriculum? Of teaching and learning? What difference does it make that Christian Story is our content? That the church is our context?

Prior to taking up these issues, however, we need to address the problematic nature of the authority of the teaching office in the contemporary Protestant church. Teaching is at the heart of Christian education, and teaching requires us to say something "on good authority."

Certainly the greatest challenge facing the Protestant church today owes to the loss of an authoritative sense of its teaching office, along with the loss of the spiritual reference of its ministry overall. Owing in large measure to the cultural captivity of religion in America, ministry today in mainline (or oldline) Protestantism lacks authority, clarity, and direction. As we have seen, the predominating paradigm for ministry is a composite of therapeutic, managerial, and organizational development values. Until the church is clearer about spirituality as the heart of Christian ministry, then evangelism, teaching, and preaching will aim for little more than "church growth," perniciously understood as swelling the membership ranks in competition with the fast-growing evangelical churches.

This book represents an attempt to explore the church's educational ministry through the prism of spirituality and formation. In particular, I want to show the inextricable link between spiritual direction and the teaching office of the church. It is the task of spiritual guidance and spiritual formation that sets *Christian* education apart from education as conventionally understood and practiced in the public sector.

In chapter 2 we explored how the pervasiveness of utilitarian and expressive individualism in modern culture undercuts the authority of the church's ministry of teaching and spiritual direction. Modern individualism appoints the individual as the final arbiter of life's meaning, value, purpose, and direction.

Individualism is not the only threat, however, to ministry in and by the mainline Protestant churches. Sociologists, such as Peter Berger, have identified and described the phenomenon of countermodernizing forces and groups that are attracting droves of individuals, especially young urban professionals.[1] These groups set themselves over against particular features of modernity. They laud authority, but the authority to which they subscribe is not subject to question or to critical investigation. It is the simple reassertion of traditional authority that is sovereignly independent of one's own sociohistorical location.[2]

Yet equally as threatening to the mainline churches is their own intramural reactionary stance against exercising any authority at all. Some of the mainline denominations, especially those that practice conciliarism, stand guilty of a glib and facile pluralism. In their efforts to display ecumenical and pluralistic commitments, the liberal corners of the church create the unfortunate impression that any authoritative teaching whatsoever of dogma and doctrine is tantamount to practicing dogmatism and indoctrination.

This stance, however, ends up leaving individuals to fend for themselves in acquiring a distinctively Christian self-identity. It leaves those persons who yearn for clear spiritual guidance prey to the very groups held so suspect by mainline Protestantism. The church must learn how it is possible, in fact, to educate and initiate persons into a strong sense of Christian self-identity in such a way that *opens* rather than closes them to interreligious dialogue and to participation in, rather than retreat from, public life.

When the church is reticent to teach with clear authority, then both the content and the delivery systems of Christian education at all levels become dominated by what sells to consumers in the marketplace. Content gets based simply on popularly expressed personal needs, as if modern people clearly know their deepest needs.

The basic problem is that too few leaders in the church understand their role as spiritual guides and as teachers, including pastors and Christian educators. Furthermore, given the huge investment of human and material resources in producing "teacher-proof" curriculum resources and the concomitant paltry investment given to teacher training and support, the subtle implication created by the church is that

Sunday school teachers themselves are a rather witless, untrustworthy lot. If that is perchance the case (which I think not!), then rather than capitalizing on curriculum, should we not address ourselves to cultivating teachers and the art of teaching and spiritual guidance?

There is no more urgent need than that of clarifying the very nature and content of the teaching office, especially as it is linked with the office of spiritual direction. This might include exploring how teaching Christianity is different from other teaching; what the gifts and graces are for Christian teaching; how to identify, train, and support teachers in the church; what it means for pastors and educators to be spiritual guides and master teachers; what the various dimensions of the teaching office are and what constitutes its authority.

This also might mean that leaders in the church would be chosen on the basis of how well they have been formed and informed by the Christian Story, rather than simply on the fact that they are experts in business, law, public schools, banking, and the like.

What do we mean by "teaching office"? The "teaching office" essentially refers to the teaching function of the church. Teaching is at the heart of Christian education. The church could not become itself without good teaching that has spiritual guidance woven into its very fabric. The whole community teaches, of course, but the church must also select and train particular persons to be teachers.

There is no agreed-upon definition of teaching, but teaching obviously is constituted by activities intended to influence learning.[3] Since we become what we *do* over a lifetime, it makes a real difference what *kind* of activities we engage in together. Teachers are ones who arrange the immediate environment and who select the specific content and experiences intended to influence learning. If this is the case, then teachers wield much power and influence in the classroom. Their personal theological persuasions, in fact, override any notion of so-called teacher-proof materials. There is no such thing! The most important curriculum is that which is already *in* teachers. Hence, we cannot afford to be haphazard in how we fill the teaching office. Articulate, faithful Christians are the best curriculum we have!

The recovery of the teaching office means we will view teaching as an expression of Christian vocation. As such, we need more clearly to identify paths of preparation for Christian teaching. We can develop liturgies and paraliturgies to recognize and celebrate our commitment to teaching. Covenants could be developed between congregations and teachers that specify responsibilities, set forth minimal expectations of teachers, and promise the ongoing support and training necessary to sustain good teaching.

TEACHING: SCIENCE OR ART?

Education in the church takes on a shape quite distinctive from conventional education in the public sector. In the curriculum planning of public education, for instance, there is widespread concern for the formulation and use of educational objectives, behaviorally defined to achieve standardized outcomes. This owes to the notion that education is science, a notion promoted at the turn of this century by figures such as John Dewey and E. L. Thorndike.

Since the aim of science is to eliminate as much subjectivity as possible, Thorndike aspired for a science of educational practice so that teachers would not have to draw on personal and subjective factors in their teaching! He thought teachers should rely on purely impersonal, objective, scientific principles of teaching and learning. Without ambiguity, Thorndike expressed his hope for educational science that "would tell every fact about everyone's intellect and character and behavior. . . . In proportion as we get such a science we shall become masters of our own souls as we now are masters of heat and light."[4]

The scientific model assumes that reality is transparent and can be manipulated to desired outcomes. It is this strategy, then, that aspires to produce teacher-proof curriculum materials! When the scientific paradigm dominates, education becomes technology that promotes the kind of learning that easily lends itself to being measured, objectified, and quantified. In the scientific or "objectivist"[5] approach to education, knowing becomes, as Parker Palmer puts it, "a spectator sport." We become detached and set over against reality "out there."

A covert spiritual deformation of self occurs in the environment created by objectivism. Teaching becomes unilateral and authoritarian. Learners are treated as proverbial empty pitchers to be filled by the teacher. The hidden curriculum in this paradigm treats knowledge as a commodity and subtly teaches students to use it to gain power, to compete, to get ahead.

The message of Christianity teaches that there is a truth we cannot control. The prevenient grace of God, the ground of all Christian education, is a mystery that grasps us and thrusts us into community. Christian spiritual formation is based on the assumption that community, interconnectedness, and interdependencey *is* the shape of reality and *is* the nature of our very being.

From this perspective, to transform education is not to find better techniques. It is, rather, to reconsider the nature of the message to be taught and learned. We must allow our subject matter to speak to us on its own terms. It is difficult to teach Christianity, but Christianity teaches! Christian truths are not objective things, says Fred Craddock, that we may simply pass around the Sunday school table much as we might pass around a bowl of potatoes at the dinner table. Christianity is a message of truth aimed to change us, especially through "I-Thou" relationships.

In becoming Christian, we are called to follow the One who says "I am the truth" and to participate in the community created by that following. In the context of Christian education, as Palmer observes, to teach is to create the environment or space where we may be grasped by truth, follow it, practice it together.[6] Critical thinking, reflection, and inquiry find their proper roles not in controlling reality but in contributing to community, in discerning how to be faithful to the One who has called us into being.

In this mode, truth is not parcelled out by the teacher, but emerges through dialogue in a covenant community that includes voices of the past and the present. Teachers and learners are partners in a whole configuration of authorities, none of whom dominates the others but each of whom is subordinate to the authority of the gospel. These authorities, to be kept in lively conversation with one another, include: pastors, professional educators, classroom teachers, ordinary Christian believers, councils, creeds, confessions, catechisms, congregations, theologians, judicatory bodies, and bishops and other church leaders.

In Christian teaching, moreover, the difference between teachers and learners begins to be one of degree once the students are on the inside of the Story. Teachers and learners alike are co-pilgrims in the shared experience of a common world, a common history, a common community. Their relationship is not based upon unequal knowledge, power, or status but upon mutuality, cooperation, and the desire to live a common Story together. Teachers are those more familiar with the twists, turns, contours, and detours of the Story; they are more skilled in finding and cutting pathways of participation. They are caring, compassionate companions along the Way.

Evaluation, thus, in terms of Christian education, is much

more elusive than in secular education. The use of learning objectives in Christian education is not a logical, straightforward listing of operationally defined objectives. It is a process of keeping an organizing image at the center of our intentions and doings.[7] If results can be measured at all, it is only as we test the spirits, discern, listen, interpret, share, and care together.

Given this perspective, teaching becomes a redemptive and artistic process. As such, Christian teaching can be characterized (1) as *evangelical,* since anyone who teaches Christianity is evangelical if he or she feels compelled by grace to share a message of good news; (2) as *invitational* in quality, reflecting a "tell me more" attitude from the teacher; (3) as *bilateral,* because teachers also learn from the unique life experiences, insights, and questions of learners; (4) as *experiential,* in that it is structured to provide learners access to their own life experiences as a resource for knowing; (5) as *dialogical* and open ended,[8] acknowledging that truth emerges in genuine conversation among multiple authorities, each relativized only by scriptural authority; (6) as *anticipatory,* in that it opens learners to welcome surprises and to envision, to embrace, and to enact God's promised future for them.

CHRISTIAN EDUCATION: THE DYNAMIC PROCESSES

Christian education can be defined as the dynamic, intentional process of teaching and learning through which the faith community is initiated into ever more faithful and complex participation in God's creative and redemptive activity in the world. It consists of three interrelated, intentional, and lifelong processes, conducted by the faith community, through which Christian character receives its distinctive shape and orientation over a lifetime and through which the church itself is more fully initiated into the Realm of God. These are *worship, praxis,* and *instruction* (fig. 9.1).

Worship is the service the church renders to God. It is not only the central event of gathering but also a pervasive posture of life sponsored by that gathering. Worship includes immersing persons in the means of grace and other spiritual disciplines.

Instruction refers to deliberate means whereby the faith community teaches the Story (Scripture and tradition) and skills for critical *inquiry* into and faithful, critical *revision* of it.

Praxis refers to the total complex of action, including theological reflection upon that action, related to the church's engagement with the stranger, people who suffer, who are in need, who are dispossessed and powerless. Praxis includes the practices (means of grace) that Wesley called works of mercy and justice.

Through *worship* we rehearse together an alternative vision of reality. Through *praxis* we flesh out that vision in the world. Through *instruction* we acquire the knowledge and skills to do so. These three processes are systematic, sustained, lifelong, organically interrelated yet distinctive.

Since worship is essentially a prereflective, uncritical incorporation into the church's Story, it must be complemented by an intentional process whereby the tradition may be critically tested and faithfully revised. The traditioning process requires far more than simple transmission, indoctrination, or blind obeisance. Traditions can live only through creative reappropriation by persons who are willing to reflect critically on their lives. Along with its transmissive function, then, critical inquiry is an important task of instruction. Transmission and revision must stand in dynamic, dialectical tension in the instructional enterprise.

An important outcome of education, thus, is the capacity to engage in prophetic judgment on one's tradition. The interrelated processes of worship, praxis, and instruction *each*

Figure 9.1.

Christian Education: Three Dynamic Processes for Christian Formation and for Initiation into the Realm of God

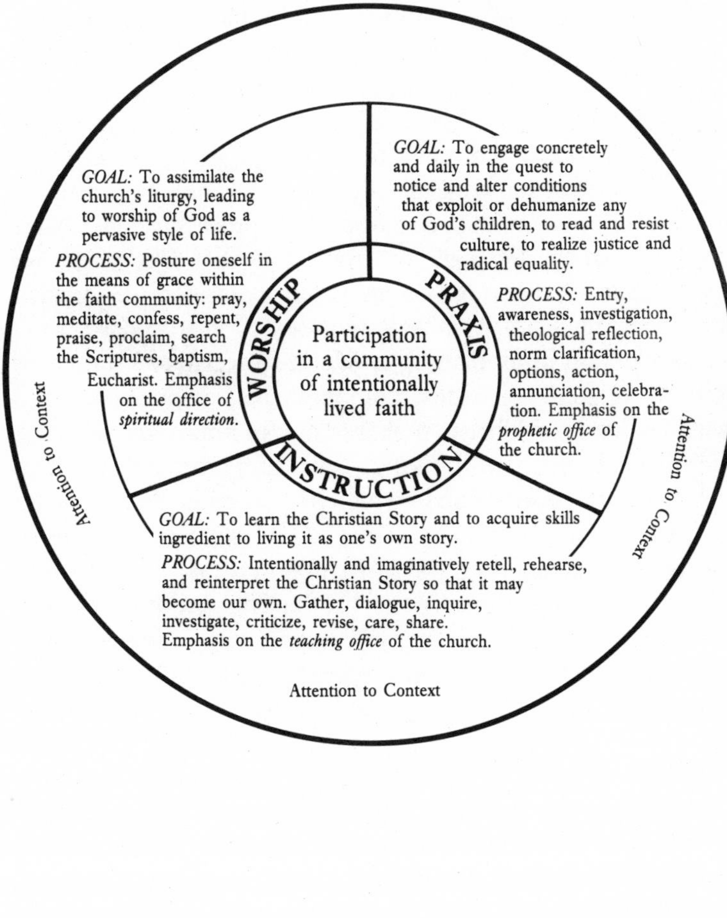

GOAL: To assimilate the church's liturgy, leading to worship of God as a pervasive style of life.

PROCESS: Posture oneself in the means of grace within the faith community: pray, meditate, confess, repent, praise, proclaim, search the Scriptures, baptism, Eucharist. Emphasis on the office of *spiritual direction.*

GOAL: To engage concretely and daily in the quest to notice and alter conditions that exploit or dehumanize any of God's children, to read and resist culture, to realize justice and radical equality.

PROCESS: Entry, awareness, investigation, theological reflection, norm clarification, options, action, annunciation, celebration. Emphasis on the *prophetic office* of the church.

WORSHIP

PRAXIS

Participation in a community of intentionally lived faith

INSTRUCTION

GOAL: To learn the Christian Story and to acquire skills ingredient to living it as one's own story.

PROCESS: Intentionally and imaginatively retell, rehearse, and reinterpret the Christian Story so that it may become our own. Gather, dialogue, inquire, investigate, criticize, revise, care, share. Emphasis on the *teaching office* of the church.

Attention to Context

Attention to Context

Attention to Context

contribute to the capacity to render prophetic judgment. Prophetic awareness derives from concrete engagement (praxis) in the struggle against specific forms of bondage, from the alternative shaping of social imagination (worship), and from critical inquiry into the tradition (instruction).

THE CHURCH INSTRUCTS

Admittedly, instruction has acquired a bad reputation in educational circles. It is mistakenly thought of as imparting an objective content that has little to do with the subjectivity of the learner. Yet Christianity is not an objective doctrine but a lived reality. It is an inner transformation.[9] As Kierkegaard expressed it, those who have either an objective or a merely socialized Christianity and none other are *eo ipso* pagan.[10]

When instruction is mistakenly understood only as transmittal of new information, then conceivably the process can take place in one's study, by mail, or from a book.[11] But when we understand Christian formation as the acquisition of Christian character, then much more is required of instruction.

Instruction aims overall to evoke in learners a range of closely related capacities, competencies, dispositions, and virtues that lend Christian character. An important outcome is practical Christian thinking. This refers to the capacity to understand the situation in which one is acting, as well as the norms by which to proceed as a Christian on any given occasion. Put another way, instruction aims, among other things, to evoke capacities of "reflective wisdom" (Farley) that include insight, vision, discernment, judgment, and action. These are all ingredient to mature Christian participation.

Modes of Instruction

Instruction is conducted through a broad range of modes woven into the educational tapestry. Two basic instructional modes include the following.

(1) *Practice* and *experience*, in which the church selects and engages persons in actions that posture them to say, to do, and to become the Story together. There is no exhaustive list of such actions, but basically they will devolve from, in Wesley's terminology, works of piety and works of mercy. Engagement in them begins quite simply, particularly with children and new converts, and becomes increasingly complex throughout a lifetime as learners assume them as their own actions.

(2) *Critical inquiry* and *investigation*, involving a cycle of basic learning tasks: (a) *listening* with growing awareness to the Christian Story; (b) *exploring* oneself and the world through the lens supplied by the Story; (c) *discovering* meaning and value for oneself within the Story, and *interpreting* oneself in light of it; (d) *appropriating* the Way of life rendered by the Story, while resisting and countering the dominant culture; (e) *assuming responsibility* to score one's whole life as well as to shape the world in accordance with images received from the Story.[12] There is an implicit developmental progression in these tasks. That is, before one can reflect upon, revise, or interpret the Story, one must be familiar with it. Christian education begins by immersing persons in the Story (Scripture and tradition). Yet in the case of young children, we would be mistaken to assume that education consists only of hearing the stories. Even children, at appropriate levels, are capable of recognizing and resisting the dominant culture.

First Comes the Story. . .

Dominant in our culture is the notion that there exists in all persons the potential for generic religious or spiritual experience. It is an arbitrary matter of personal taste as to what religious tradition, if any at all, shall then be chosen to express that common core experience. In *The Nature of Doctrine*, George Lindbeck describes this position as the "experiential-expressivist" theory of religion.[13]

This theory underwrites religious education based upon structural-developmental thought (or upon *eudaimonism*) where a specific content makes little difference to religious growth and change. Religious education in this mode rests largely on drawing something out of persons, not putting something into them. It does this through experiential over against content-based education.

Lindbeck argues that this position is naïve and reductionistic. It is necessary, he says, to have some means of recognizing and expressing experience *in order to have it.* Means of expressing experience with God is the a priori condition for having experience in the first place. The richer the language and the symbols conveyed to us, the richer the experiences we are able to have.

Just as it is ridiculous to say that one can speak language in general, Lindbeck notes, it is ridiculous to say that one can be spiritual or religious *in general!* Language, symbol, and belief systems not only express spiritual experience, but they also *propose* it and *form* it. Particular symbols afford particular experiences. There are countless thoughts we cannot think, countless sentiments we cannot hold, countless realities we cannot perceive, unless we have learned, through instruction, how to use the appropriate symbol system.[14]

Church teachings and the range of materials included in the metaphor of Christian Story function first and foremost as ways to pattern who we are and what we do, not merely express. The Story acts on us first to shape our subjectivities, attitudes, and actions. The primary knowledge to be conveyed by Christian education is not *about* Christianity or *that* Christianity teaches thus and so, but rather *how* to be Christian in such and such ways.[15]

In the formation perspective, then, experience is vitally important, but *first* comes the Story, to be made accessible in the teaching activity of the church. The Story always remains somewhat independent of us; we cannot completely control its normative power. Innovation, creativity, and critique are possible only *after* one has become interior to the tradition. In Kierkegaard's terms, this is because "Christianity exists before any Christian exists, it must exist in order that one may become Christian, it contains the determinant by which one may test whether one has become a Christian, it maintains its objective subsistence apart from all believers, while at the same time it is the inwardness of the believer."[16]

Christian formation thus begins in an a priori acceptance of authority and instruction that transforms our experience and determines our character.[17] First we must decide to become Christian. Next we must submit ourselves to prolonged instruction and initiation. We must give ourselves over to the Story, begin to participate in it; only then do we really begin to understand! *Credo ut intelligam:* "I participate fully in order that I might understand."

When conducted within the above perspective, instructional activity will aim to (1) acquaint persons with or reintroduce them to Jesus Christ; (2) convey to young people and adult converts the basic Christian witness of faith, in continuity with the original message of Jesus and the apostolic church; (3) help persons to interpret, to understand, and to live in light of the Christian Story; (4) teach skills of critical inquiry into Scripture and tradition; (5) teach Christians the skills of critical engagement with culture (praxis), so that they can help shape the public; (6) immerse believers in and help them reflect upon their experience of the means of grace; (7) help believers originate their own witness to the good news, rather than remain as passive recipients of someone else's witness.

THE CHURCH ENGAGES IN PRAXIS

Authentic Christian spirituality, according to the biblical witness, cannot emerge apart from struggling together against particular powers and principalities in our given sociocultural context (Eph. 6:12). Spiritual existence requires that we refuse interpersonal, social, or economic arrangements that deny life to us or to any of God's children. Christian spirituality compels us not only to search out and embrace the stranger but also to search out and address systems and structures that estrange, alienate, and dehumanize.

Because we have not learned to think sociologically or culturally, we abstract persons from the cultural, historical matrix that profoundly affects their entire self-identity and self-understanding. Instead, we construct everything as an individual, intrapsychic issue. We thus fail to see how deeply affected we are, at all levels, by the systems and structures in which we dwell. Our call today is to liberate Christian spirituality from its isolationist, individualistic and otherworldly moorings. It must be rooted in our common life. And, it must lock horns with cultural conditions that do not promote the values of God's Realm. We must not only teach persons how to read the Bible, but also how to read and resist their dominant culture.

This task requires a process of raising critical consciousness. Critical awareness is not achieved simply through intellectual striving. It requires confession and repentance, along with entering into solidarity with those who suffer, and a willingness to be changed by that engagement. Critical consciousness leads us to recognize our complicity in conditions that dehumanize and that isolate persons who are different. Further, it leads us to struggle collectively against these conditions and, finally, to refuse decay and bondage as the last word on human existence.

There are various ways to concretely engage in Christian praxis. Katie Cannon calls our visible, tangible praxis the "dance of redemption," and Beverly Harrison offers specific, identifiable steps for it in *Making the Connections*.[18]

Steps in the Divine Dance of Redemption

1. Consciousness raising is the entry point into shared Christian praxis. It begins in collective storytelling. When we name with others our experience, what seemed originally to be an individual problem is exposed as a basic pattern affecting all society. Each person discovers that she or he is not alone.

2. Historical-contextual investigation is a process of connecting our particular experiences to a larger historical framework. Christian education is a matter of helping specific faith communities inquire into the church's experience as seen in its Scripture, in its historic experience, and in its present and varied circumstances. This phase takes with utmost seriousness the given cultural context of a specific faith community, seeking to understand the dynamics and forces at work within that immediate context as well as the wider world. It asks how the church's past as well as present experience elsewhere in the world can illumine the search for faithfulness here and now.

The past, of course, is not a "treasure trove" of easy formulas, right actions, perfect solutions, but it does bear stories of human courage, hope, and dignity. The historical-contextual perspective empowers us in several ways. First, we see how the past has come to put certain restraints on us, partially as the result of collective human agency. Second, we form a redemptive memory as we see how our forebears may have resisted sin and oppression. Third, when we listen to faith communities other than our own, we begin to have our own blind spots corrected.

3. Theological reflection seeks not merely to reassert traditional theology but to ask whether and how the theological tradition offers a genuinely liberating word for a specific community. The community conducts theological reflection by engaging with Scripture and tradition in light of its present socio-cultural situation.[19]

4. Norm clarification is the movement wherein, in light of our theological reflection, norms are generated, clarified, weighed, and used as guides to choices. Norms are conditioned by our struggle in a specific cultural context. For Harrison, norms are grounded in a radically relational understanding of human justice. Justice can be defined as "rightly ordered relationships of mutuality" set within the total network of social reality.[20] Norms provide us general directions rather than specific actions.

5. Strategic options for action must be generated, calculating their possible long-term consequences. This phase must not be allowed to degenerate into myopic short-term thinking about what "works" in the immediate sense. Our approach must be tempered by ongoing, long-term loyalty to a particular people. Though actions must be realistic and concrete, they should reflect hopeful imagination.

6. Annunciation and celebration is the reconstructive phase of shared Christian praxis, possible only after our self-conscious critique of society, dominant culture, and tradition. We annunciate and celebrate the inbreaking Realm of God, which is our original source of motivation. Spirituality is authenticated as together we worship and celebrate the God who sustains our struggle together.[21]

7. Reorientation and reentry, along with reengagement, carry us further into the divine dance of redemption. We continue the ever-spiraling circle of shared Christian praxis. Having collectively discovered its power, we become all the more hopeful for the fullness of God's Realm when justice rolls down like water.

Though this description of shared Christian praxis may at first glance seem otherwise, it is definitely not an exercise for the intellectually elite. It is, in fact, a process that is going on among communities of common people in Central American and in third world settings. These are coming to be known as base ecclesial communities. In these settings, even the illiterate gather to ponder the Bible, to look at their concrete situation, to share their experience of the land and of being poor, and to listen together for God's Word. They learn from the struggles of their ancestors, and they try to envision concrete ways of realizing their Christian hope.

The process essentially lies in helping persons to give voice to their experience in light of the biblical message and to ask what it means for resisting and countering the dominant culture.

Carlos Mesters writes about his experience with illiterate farmers from the backlands and riverbanks in northeast Brazil. "What does the Bible say about our fight for land?" they asked. "The landlord gives catechetical lessons that teach us to be subservient. Is this right?" "Tell us stories about Abraham, Moses, Jeremiah and Jesus," they said.

As Mesters points out, these farmers struggle to integrate and interrelate the Bible (text), their specific community (context), and the reality of their real-life situation in a surrounding world (pre-text). Their purpose is to hear the word of God for them today, and to respond in faithfulness. The Christian witness of faith, the community, and historical reality are all introduced into the process of interpretation.[22]

Even young children can question, inquire, interpret, and resist the world in which they live, suggests Dykstra.[23] In illustrating this point, Dykstra recounts a passage from Robert Cole's book *The Moral Life of Children*. The story is about Ruby Bridges, a young black child who, with the help of federal marshals, braved her way through screaming, spitting, angry adults to integrate a school in New Orleans . . . at age six! How could she do it!? Coles asked her. She replied that every night before she went to sleep she prayed for the people who would be there in the morning to revile her. But why did she do it? "I go to church every Sunday, and we're told to pray for everyone, even the bad people, and so I do."

If the church is to take seriously God's redemptive activity in the world, then the church will help its members find where that activity is going on and assist them in participating in it. This will mean looking within our own congregations for people who are different or disabled, who are in need, who struggle and suffer. But also it will mean looking beyond our own homogeneity, actively searching for the hidden pockets of poverty, hunger, loneliness, and isolation. It may mean taking young people to soup kitchens and city council meetings, taking adults to prisons and halfway houses, taking children to nursing homes. Above all, it will mean getting believers out of the church building and into places where they can serve as neighbors to those laying beside the road of life.

SUMMARY

As conceived in this work, Christian spiritual formation is the decisive guiding aim, motive, or outcome of Christian education. Formation itself is not a deliberate activity. It is, rather, the hoped-for outcome of the deliberate activities of worship, praxis, and instruction in the educational enterprise.

The model of formation presented here can help overcome the false dichotomy between education as inner self-development (experiential education) and education as *traditio* (transmitting content).[24] At stake is the creative tension between drawing something out of the person *(eudaimonism)*, *characteristically a liberal approach, and putting something into the person (traditio)*, a more conservative approach. The former educates from the inside out and the latter from the outside in. Formation can be seen as a postliberal approach that synthesizes and overcomes long-existing false dualisms.

The Socratic notion of "drawing out" is the educational

implication of developmental psychologies. Experiential-developmental approaches reflect classic romanticism and idealism (à la Rousseau), which emphasize the innate goodness in human nature. They simply seek to help it blossom through education. Unfortunately, such romantic theories ignore the reality of human sin and self-deception. R. S. Peters thus argues that it is not enough for education merely to draw out an individual's given aspirations. The educator would not want to develop the natural inclinations of a Marquis de Sade!

Christian education is more a matter of initiating persons into a Story than it is of drawing something out of them. Moreover, the Christian Story is less a confirmation and more a critique of our given tendencies. The Story claims to help expose and clear away our sin and self-deception.

Unfortunately, we have tended to associate the *imago Dei* with the *daimon* or the drive toward self-actualization. Yet the *imago Dei* is actually a relational, communal metaphor, whereas the *daimon* is an individualistic, private one. The *imago Dei* is a way to talk about our call to participate in the inner life of God. It is not a call to concentrate on getting ourselves changed. We are called to follow Jesus Christ and enter his Story, and to participate in the community created by that following. And this does, after all, change us, as we ourselves become as the Story is.

Epilogue

Throughout the previous chapters, we have emphasized the following major points concerning Christian spiritual formation:

1. Formation begins with our baptism into a community of intentionally lived faith and relies upon the formative and transformative power of the congregation throughout a lifetime.

2. Formation places equal emphasis upon both content and process (or experience). Whereas a liberal approach tends to emphasize process/experience and a conservative approach content, formation as a postliberal approach seeks to overcome the age-old dualism, partially by reconceiving the nature and function of the content to be taught.

3. Formation is a lifelong affair involving highly complex, organically related processes and content, a partial list of which includes

- exemplars, spiritual guides, role models, official and "ordinary" saints of the church, faith relationships between individuals of different generations
- dialogue, critical inquiry, interpretation, reflection, and feedback within a community of care and guidance

- the church's internal life, including its polity, administration, supervision, leadership, politics, and how the organizational elements either empower or disenfranchise active participation in the church's worship, witness, and work
- attitudes, affections, and actions appropriate to Christian character, demonstrated and supported in the faith community
- "functional apprenticeships" wherein young people and catechumens are given opportunities to establish relationships with faith mentors, wherein each of us is given opportunity to develop and exercise leadership skills, wherein each of us is shown models of vocation and helped to discover his or her own unique path to vocation and discipleship
- liturgy and paraliturgy where the Story is dramatized and rehearsed through ritual, rite, silence, and song
- spiritual disciplines, including the means of grace and works of mercy as we are immersed and trained in them and helped to practice and reflect upon them together in groups marked by covenant relationship
- environmental influences that are *both* explicit and hidden, including all the formal and informal enculturation processes of the church as it engages in its worship, work, and witness
- language and symbols—acquired through worship, instruction, and praxis—that instill values in us and that shape us to see and do *this* rather than *that*
- critical inquiry into Scripture and tradition, including critical appropriation and revision of the church's common memory

4. Formation includes equal emphasis on worship, praxis, and instruction as the dynamic, organically related, and interlocking processes of Christian education. Formation

places equal emphasis on critical reflection, along with prereflective, experiential activity. Learners both act on and are acted on by the church and its decisive Story.

5. Formation places equal emphasis on the individual and the community. They are held in dialectical, dynamic tension and neither is given primacy over the other.

6. Formation is intimately concerned with shaping our subjectivity as individuals, our attitudes and affections. The locus of formation is character, involving the orientation of our intentions/actions, the shape of our virtues and deepest heartfelt desires, the congruity between our behaviors and beliefs.

7. Formation equips us to be critically self-aware of the culture in which we participate and to know the difference between the Christian Story and the many stories of our culture that bid for our commitment and loyalty. It equips us for interreligious, ecumenical dialogue and engenders our commitment to help shape, rather than simply be shaped by or retreat from, the public.

8. Formation requires a community that is intentional and disciplined in its spiritual life and that includes in the process of Christian initiation training in prayer and meditation, searching the Scriptures, repentance and confession, praise and proclamation, works of mercy and justice.

9. Formation depends upon the authoritative exercise of the offices of spiritual direction, teaching, and prophetic judgment.

10. Formation involves more than self-development (pulling innate goodness out of us); it is concerned with clearing away self-deception and sin and putting something into us (through worship, praxis and instruction).

Where to Begin

As congregations become interested in spiritual formation, they are tempted to begin offering new programs and new classes alongside their already existing educational programs. This adds to the unfortunate impression that spirituality is a "thing" apart from Christian formation. But spiritual formation simply cannot be understood apart from Christian formation.

The place to begin, therefore, is by looking at how our congregations already sponsor Christian formation. The creation of new settings is not the best way to begin. There will always be Sunday school, worship, fellowship dinners, administrative decisions, visitation, marrying, burying, counseling. Rich opportunities for teaching and for spiritual guidance exist already in these settings. The faith community can clarify, celebrate, and extend the spiritual guidance intrinsic to them. Bringing persons to a new, fresh hearing of the good news links spiritual care with Christian teaching in such settings.

Fred Craddock rightly acknowledges that "whether we teach or preach or both, we have no more urgent or important or demanding task than that of effecting a new hearing of the gospel."[1] The content of Christian formation is the old, old Story, retold, reinterpreted, and rehearsed so that modern men and women may hear afresh its transformative good news. The invitation of the Story is to *participate*, not simply to *memorize*. But as Craddock laments, unfortunately teaching and preaching in the church "are seldom seen as producing, contributing to the continuation of the discourse we call 'the story,' but more often as consuming, using parts of the story already easily available for a sermon or lesson."[2]

The hermeneutics of participation remind us of the urgency of biblical preaching and teaching but transform the way we approach these tasks. We are to tell the Story so as to invite and empower learners to participate in the drama and action it reveals. We are not only to read the Story but also to pray the Story, to sing the Story, to paint and dance the Story, to meditate on it and savor it through *lectio divina*, to rehearse it in liturgy and paraliturgy, to enact it through works of mercy and justice, and to hold one another accountable to it through covenantal groups.

Renewal of spiritual care, of Christian initiation, and of the teaching office of the church holds out revolutionary significance for the life of the Protestant church in America. Nothing less will form Christians who have a clear and articulate sense of self-definition in the modern milieu of pluralism. Participation in the global village requires that we have something decisive to contribute. Authentic ecumenical dialogue requires that persons be more, not less, decisively formed by their respective traditions.

The time is ripe in mainline Protestant churches for us to renew our vision of education and ministry overall. We cannot afford to be anything less than a community capable of forming persons with character and virtues sufficient to provide a compelling witness to the new Way of living whose advent is Jesus Christ. Increasing numbers of persons in contemporary culture are searching for a way to commit themselves to a community radically distinct from the prevailing culture.

Christian education stands at a critical crossroads in charting its direction into a new century. It is hoped that this discussion will contribute to a sense of excitement for new directions, as well as stimulate some ecumenical dialogue and insights as to what our real possibilities are.

Notes

Introduction

1. In this work, I am less concerned with spirituality as a general phenomenon than as it is distinctively Christian in its orientation. I assume that the intent of *Christian* education is to form Christians, not people who are religious in general (in fact, there is no such thing). This is not to deny the truthfulness of other religious narratives but to reaffirm that we reach the universal through our own particular existence.

2. For a historical tracing of the word "spirituality," see Walter Principe, "Toward Defining Spirituality" *Sciences Religieuses/Studies in Religion* 12, no. 2 (Spring 1983):127-41.

3. Gustavo Gutierrez, *We Drink from Our Own Wells: The Spiritual Journey of a People* (Maryknoll, N.Y.: Orbis Press, 1984).

4. Don E. Saliers, *Worship and Spirituality* (Philadelphia: Westminster Press, 1984), pp. 17-18.

5. *Ibid.*, p. 25.

1. Drinking from Our Own Wells: An Introduction

1. Clifford Geertz, "Religion as a Cultural System," in *The Religious Situation: 1968*, Vol. I, Donald R. Cutler (Boston: Beacon Press, 1968), p. 664.

2. Jacques Ellul, *Hope in Time of Abandonment,* trans. C. Edward Hopkin (New York: Seabury Press, 1977).

3. Douglas John Hall, "Beyond Cynicism and Credulity: On the Meaning of Christian Hope," *The Princeton Seminary Bulletin* 6, no. 3 (1985): 201-10.

4. Fred B. Craddock, *Overhearing the Gospel* (Nashville: Abingdon Press, 1978), p. 18.

5. Eugen Rosenstock-Huessey, *Out of Revolution: Autobiography of Western Man* (New York: Four Wells, 1964), p. 4.

6. As a theological ethicist, Hauerwas claims that the first moral questions we ask must revolve around the sort of community and history to which we wish to belong. Cf. Stanley Hauerwas, *A Community of Character: Toward A Constructive Christian Social Ethic* (Notre Dame, Ind.: University of Notre Dame Press, 1981), p. 100.

7. H. Richard Niebuhr, *The Meaning of Revelation* (New York: Macmillan, 1941), p. 52.

8. These assumptions owe in large measure to the influence of Stanley Hauerwas. In addition to *A Community of Character,* see the following: *Vision and Virtue: Essays in Christian Ethical Reflection* (Notre Dame, Ind.: University of Notre Dame Press, 1981); *Truthfulness and Tragedy: Further Investigations in Christian Ethics* (Notre Dame, Ind.: University of Notre Dame Press, 1977); *Character and the Christian Life: A Study in Theological Ethics* (San Antonio: Trinity University Press, 1975).

9. Matthew Fox, *Original Blessing* (Santa Fe, N. Mex.: Bear and Co., 1983). For a summary of the way Fox contrasts "redemption" and "creation" spiritualities, see his Appendix B, pp. 316-19. One can see at a glance how Fox caricatures redemption spirituality. Many of the motifs he sides with creation theology rightly belong to the concerns of redemption theology, especially in the biblical witness (cf. Isa. 65:17-23; Ps. 107). The prophetic-eschatological tradition to which Jesus belonged included redemption and creation motifs. Rather than that which is truly redemption based, Fox essentially reacts against the very worst side of the classical *ascetical* tradition in spirituality.

10. See Letty Russell, *Household of Freedom* (Philadelphia: Westminster Press, 1987).

11. Carol Ochs, *Women and Spirituality* (Totowa, N.J.: Rowman and Allanheld, 1983), p. 134.

12. Susan Cady, with Marian Ronan and Hal Taussig, *Sophia: The Future of Feminist Spirituality* (San Francisco: Harper & Row, 1986), p. 5.

13. See autobiographical statements by Elizabeth Schussler-Fiorenza in "Feminist Spirituality, Christian Identity and Catholic Vision," in *Womanspirit Rising*, ed. Carol P. Christ and Judith Plaskow (San Francisco: Harper & Row, 1979), p. 137.

14. Austin Farrer, *A Rebirth of Images* (Boston: Beacon Press, 1949), p. 14.

15. Daniel Migliore, *Called to Freedom: Liberation Theology and the Future of Christian Doctrine* (Philadelphia: Westminster Press, 1980), p. 90.

16. For attention to the concept of participation, see also James N. Lapsley, *Salvation and Health: The Interlocking Processes of Life* (Philadelphia: Westminster Press, 1972); Fred B. Craddock, *Overhearing the Gospel* (Nashville: Abingdon Press, 1978); Craig Dykstra, "No Longer Strangers: The Church and Its Educational Ministry," *Princeton Seminary Bulletin* 6, no. 3 (1985): 188-200.

17. Harry Guntrip, "Psychology and Spirituality," in *Spirituality for Today*, ed. Eric James (London: SCM Press, 1968), p. 98.

18. Craddock, *Overhearing the Gospel*. See chapter 1 which is an exposition of this passage for the theoretical focus of the book.

19. *Ibid.*, p. 31.

20. *Ibid.*, pp. 27-28.

2. Drinking from Other Wells: A Partial Critique

1. Daniel Yankelovich defines psycho-culture as the web of meanings Americans hold in common that focus exclusively on inner psychological processes. See Yankelovich, *New Rules: Searching for Self-Fulfillment in a World Turned Upside Down* (New York: Random House, 1981), p. 14.

2. Don Browning addresses this basic question to the culture at large. I wish to address it to the church. For ideas and insights in this chapter, I am deeply indebted to the ongoing work of Browning, especially that in his most recent book, *Religious Thought*

and the Modern Psychologies (Philadelphia: Fortress Press, 1987).
3. To begin with, we wonder about the kind of world we live in and what its ultimate context is (the *visional* or *metaphorical* level). Based on the world we see through metaphors and myths, we ask about what we are obliged to do and to be within this world (the *obligational* level). Third, we wonder about the basic human needs that we should seek to satisfy within ourselves (the *tendency-need* level). See Browning, *Religious Thought*, chapter 1.
4. David L. Norton, *Personal Destinies: A Philosophy of Ethical Individualism* (Princeton, N.J.: Princeton University Press, 1976), pp. 5-6.
5. Browning, *Religious Thought*, p. 72.
6. Phillip Rieff, *The Triumph of the Therapeutic: Uses of Faith after Freud* (London: Chattor Windus, 1966).
7. Robert N. Bellah, Richard Modsen, William M. Sullivan, Ann Swidler, and Steven M. Tipton, *Habits of the Heart: Individualism and Commitment in American Life* (Berkeley: University of California Press, 1985), p. 47.
8. See Don Saliers, *The Soul in Paraphrase: Prayer and the Religious Affections* (New York: Seabury Press, 1980) for a helpful discussion of "holy fear" as a vital aspect of Christian religious affections and Christian spirituality (reminiscent of Otto's discussion of the *mysterium tremendum*).
9. Bellah et al., *Habits*, p. 47.
10. Ruth Tiffany Barnhouse, "Spiritual Direction and Psychotherapy," *Journal of Pastoral Care*, 33, no. 3 (September 1979): 149.
11. Bellah, *Habits*, p. 47.
12. Jean Bethke Elshtain, "The Self: Reborn, Undone, Transformed," *Telos* 44 (Summer 1980): 102.
13. Bellah et al., *Habits*, p. 6.
14. Susan Thistlethwaite, *Metaphors for the Contemporary Church* (New York: Pilgrim Press, 1983), p. 112.

3. Participation: Theological Foundations

1. Cf. Isaiah 2:2-4; 25:6-9; 35:1-10; 58:6-7, 9*a*-11; 65:17-25; Psalms 98:1-3; 146:5-10; Jeremiah 31:33-34; Matthew 19:16-21; 20:1-16; Mark 4:1-33; Luke 14:7-24.

2. Paul Lehman, *Ethics in a Christian Context* (New York: Harper & Row, 1963), pp. 117-23.
3. Mother Teresa, *Life in the Spirit: Reflections, Meditations, Prayers,* ed. Kathryn Spink (San Francisco: Harper & Row, 1983), p. 16.
4. Ibid., p. 13.
5. Russell, *Household,* p. 84.
6. Hauerwas, *A Community,* p. 49.
7. Schubert Ogden, *The Point of Christology* (San Francisco: Harper & Row, 1982), p. 123.
8. Letty Russell, *The Future of Partnership* (Philadelphia: Westminster Press, 1979), p. 71.
9. Lehman, *Ethics,* p. 122.
10. James F. White, *Sacraments as God's Self-Giving: Sacramental Practice and Faith* (Nashville: Abingdon Press, 1983), p. 93.
11. Russell, *The Future,* p. 153.
12. White, *Sacraments,* passim.
13. Ibid., p. 36.
14. Ibid., pp. 36-42.

4. Participation: Practical Foundations

1. John Wesley, "The Means of Grace," Sermon 16 in *The Works of John Wesley,* Vol. 1, ed. Albert C. Outler (Nashville: Abingdon Press, 1984), p. 381.
2. Gabriel Fackre, *The Christian Story: A Narrative Interpretation of Basic Christian Doctrine* (Grand Rapids, Mich.: Eerdman's, 1984), p. 184.
3. Ibid.
4. Paul S. Minear, *Images of the Church in the New Testament* (Philadelphia: Westminster Press, 1960), p. 172.
5. White, *Sacraments,* p. 93.
6. John Wesley, "The Scripture Way of Salvation," in Albert C. Outler, *Works of John Wesley,* (New York: Oxford University Press, 1964), p. 280.
7. Ibid.
8. White, *Sacraments,* p. 95.
9. Martin Buber, *Hasidism and Modern Man* (New York: Harper & Row, 1966), p. 140.

10. Walter Brueggemann, "Covenanting as Human Vocation: A Discussion of the Relation of the Bible and Pastoral Care," *Interpretation* 33, no. 2 (April 1979): 125.

11. Ibid., p. 116.

12. The normal and technical meaning of the word "liturgy" *(leitourgia)* in classical Greek is that of public service, a function exercised in the interests of all the people, whether it be in a religious, technical, or political realm. See H. Strathmann, "Leitourgeo, leitourgia, leitourgos, leitourgikos," in *Theological Dictionary of the New Testament*, Vol. IV, ed. Gerhard Kittel (Grand Rapids, Mich.: Eerdmans, 1964), pp. 216-15. See also K. L. Smidt, "Ekklesia," *Theological Dictionary*, Vol. III, pp. 501-6.

13. John Howard Yoder, *The Priestly Kingdom: Social Ethics as Gospel* (Notre Dame, Ind.: University of Notre Dame Press, 1984), p. 43.

14. Richard J. Foster, *Celebration of Discipline: The Path to Spiritual Growth* (London: Hodder and Stoughton, 1984), p. 148.

15. Saliers, *The Soul in Paraphrase*, p. 51.

16. Karl Barth, *Church Dogmatics IV/1*, trans. G. W. Bromiley (Edinburgh: T&T Clark, 1957), pp. 41-42, as quoted in Saliers, *The Soul in Paraphrase*, p. 54.

17. Don E. Saliers, "Prayer and Emotion: Shaping and Expressing Christian Life," in *Christians at Prayer*, ed. John Gallen, S. J. (Notre Dame, Ind.: University of Notre Dame Press, 1977), p. 46.

18. Simone Weil, *Waiting for God*, trans. Emma Craufurd, intro. by Leslie A. Fiedler (New York: Putnam, 1951), p. 105.

19. Nathan Mitchell, "Useless Prayer," in Gallen, *Christians at Prayer*; see also David Burrell, "Prayer as the Language of the Soul," *Soundings* (Winter 1977): 388-400.

20. Gustavo Gutierrez, *A Theology of Liberation*, trans. Sister Caridad Inda and John Eagleson (Maryknoll, N.Y.: Orbis Books, 1973), p. 206.

21. Saliers, *Worship and Spirituality*, chapter 5, passim.

22. Ibid.

5. Participation: Church as Context

1. See Minear, *Images of the Church*.

2. Paul employs diverse images to describe the *ecclesia*. The writer

of Ephesians uses the term nine times: 1:22; 3:10, 21; 5:23, 24, 25, 27, 29, 32. *Ecclesia* means both the universal community and the local congregation of believers.

3. Edward Farley, *Ecclesial Man* (Philadelphia: Fortress Press, 1976). See chap. 6.

4. There is no unanimity of agreement among scholars as to the authorship of Ephesians. There are numerous literary style problems. This book does not assume Pauline authorship of Ephesians but rather leaves that as an open issue to be investigated and concluded by the reader. Throughout my discussion of Ephesians in this chapter, I rely heavily on the work of Marcus Barth, who does in fact grant Pauline authorship. See Marcus Barth, *Ephesians*, 2 vols., Anchor Bible Commentary, (Garden City, N.Y.: Doubleday, 1974).

5. Ephesians 1:22-23; 2:19-21; 3:14-21; 4:11-16; 5:25-29.

6. The terms "strangers" and "sojourners" possibly describe two legally differentiated groups. A "stranger" could be treated as an outlaw or spy (Gen. 19:1-10), and a "sojourner" was a resident alien, subject to only a portion of the law and thereby enjoying only corresponding legal protection (Lev. 25). See Barth, *Ephesians*, Vol. 1-3, p. 268.

7. The term *mysterion* plays a great role in Ephesians, occurring six times there but not with the same meaning as found in I Corinthians *(mysteria)* and other writings. *Mysterion* is not a fixed divine plan, not magic ritual or performance, not a secret communication or esoteric knowledge, not blind fate. The term *mysterion* is used to signify that God's secret is now being communicated to all the world: Gentiles are received into full membership of God's elect; they are children of God's own household. The mystery is simply that Christ is among Gentiles and Jews alike!

8. See Nils Dahl, "Interpreting Ephesians: Then and Now," *Currents in Theology and Mission* 5, no. 3 (June 1978):133-43.

9. Barth, *Ephesians*, Vols. 1-3, p. 273.

10. David Kelsey, *The Uses of Scripture in Recent Theology* (Philadelphia: Fortress Press, 1975), p. 93.

11. Karl Barth, *The Christian Life, Church Dogmatics* IV/4: *Lecture*

Fragments, trans. Geoffrey W. Bromiley (Grand Rapids, Mich.: Eerdman's, 1981), p. 95.

12. Howard Grimes, *The Church Redemptive* (New York: Abingdon Press, 1958), p. 18.

13. Craig R. Dykstra, "No Longer Strangers: The Church and Its Educational Ministry," *Princeton Seminary Bulletin* 6, no. 3 (November 1985): 195.

14. Craig Dkystra, "The Formative Power of Congregations," *Princeton Seminary Bulletin* 82, no. 4 (Fall, 1987): 530-46.

15. Ibid., pp. 533-534.

16. David Elkind, *The Hurried Child: Growing Up Too Fast Too Soon* (Reading, Mass.: Addison-Wesley, 1981), p. 129.

17. Dykstra, "The Formative Power," pp. 540-41.

18. Hauerwas, *A Community*, p. 168.

19. John Westerhoff, *Living the Faith Community* (Minneapolis: Winston Press, 1985), p. 6.

20. Markus Barth, *The Broken Wall: A Study of the Epistle to the Ephesians* (Chicago: Judson Press, 1959), p. 43.

21. Farley, *Ecclesial Man*, p. 170.

22. John Koenig, *New Testament Hospitality: Partnership with Strangers as Promise and Mission* (Philadelphia: Fortress Press, 1985), passim.

23. White, *Sacraments*, p. 96.

24. Ibid., p. 99.

25. Russell, *The Future*, p. 68.

26. Ibid., p. 147.

6. Participation: Story as Content

1. William J. Bausch, *Storytelling: Imagination and Faith* (Mystic, Conn.: Twenty-Third Publications, 1984), p. 171.

2. Barbara Hardy, "Towards a Poetics of Fiction: An Approach through Narrative," *Novel* 2 (Fall 1968): 5, as quoted in Brian Wicker, *The Story-Shaped World: Fiction and Metaphysics, Some Variations on a Theme* (Notre Dame, Ind.: University of Notre Dame Press, 1975), p. 47.

3. Gabriel Marcel, *Mystery of Being*, Vol. I, (London: Harvill Press, 1950), chapter 8, p. 148ff.

4. Ann Brennan, "Myth in Personal Spirituality," *Religious Education* 75, no. 4 (July-August 1980): 443.

5. Fackre, *The Christian Story*, p. 5.

6. Craddock, *Overhearing*, p. 16.

7. Kelsey, *The Uses of Scripture*, p. 48.

8. George Lindbeck, *The Nature of Doctrine: Religion and Theology in a Postliberal Age* (Philadelphia: Westminster Press, 1984), p. 120.

9. Craddock, *Overhearing*, p. 75.

10. Phyllis Bird addresses this issue in *The Bible as the Church's Book* (Philadelphia: Westminster Press, 1982); cf. p. 68.

11. Ibid., p. 69.

12. Walter Brueggemann, *Hope Within History* (Atlanta: John Knox Press, 1987), p. 8.

13. Bird, *The Bible*, see pp. 80ff.

14. Stanley Hauerwas, "The Gesture of a Truthful Story: The Church and 'Religious Education,'" *Encounter* 43 (Autumn 1982): 325.

15. The first three influential approaches to the Scriptures in modern Christianity are discussed by Daniel Migliore; I have added two more obstacles to his list. See Migliore, *Called to Freedom*, pp. 24-27.

16. See Phyllis Bird, *The Bible*, p. 46.

17. Hermeneutics derives from the Greek verb *hermeneuein*, meaning "to interpret," and has evolved into a broad field of study informed by philosophy, language, epistemology, psychology, and other disciplines that study and interpret the nature of human reality.

18. Stephen Crites, "The Narrative Quality of Experience," *Journal of the American Academy of Religion* 39 (1971): 310.

19. Thomas Groome, *Christian Religious Education: Sharing our Story and Vision* (San Francisco: Harper & Row, 1980).

20. Craddock, *Overhearing*, p. 133.

21. Ibid., p. 91.

22. Lindbeck, *The Nature of Doctrine*, p. 117.

23. Ibid., p. 118.

24. Fackre, *The Christian Story*, p. 13.

25. Lindbeck, *The Nature of Doctrine*, p. 121.

26. Bausch, *Storytelling*, p. 16.

27. Hauerwas, *Truthfulness and Tragedy*, p. 98.
28. Lindbeck, *The Nature of Doctrine*, p. 117.
29. Sigmund Freud, *Letters of Sigmund Freud*, ed. Ernest L. Freud (New York, 1960), p. 308, as quoted in Reiff, *The Triumph*, p. 261.
30. Sallie McFague, *Metaphorical Theology: Models of God in Religious Language* (Philadelphia: Fortress Press, 1982), p. 47.
31. Douglas J. Hall, "Beyond Cynicism and Credulity," p. 208.
32. Kelsey, *The Uses of Scriptures*, p. 44.
33. *Ibid.*, p. 46.
34. Elisabeth Schussler-Fiorenza, "The Will to Choose or to Reject: Continuing Our Critical Work," in *Feminist Interpretation of the Bible*, ed. Letty M. Russell, Phliadelphia: Westminster Press, 1985), p. 130.
35. Migliore, *Called to Freedom*, p. 35.

7. Christian Spiritual Formation

1. Matthew Arnold, *The Strayed Reveller and Other Poems* (London: B. Fellowes, 1849), as quoted in Rieff, *The Triumph*, p. 66.
2. Hauerwas, *Vision and Virtue*, p. 115.
3. Karl Barth, "The Gospel and Education," unpublished seminar paper, 1938. My thanks to my colleague John Deschner for sharing this paper with me.
4. Ibid., p. 5.
5. Jack Seymour and Donald L. Miller, *Contemporary Approaches to Christian Education* (Nashville: Abingdon Press, 1982).
6. For the most complete exposition of this theory, see James Fowler, *Stages of Faith: The Psychology of Human Development and the Quest for Meaning* (San Francisco: Harper & Row, 1981).
7. See Mary Ford-Grabowsky, "Flaws in Faith-Development Theory," *Religious Education* 82, no. 1 (Winter 1987): 81.
8. Ford-Grabowsky, "Flaws," p. 85.
9. Ibid.
10. I owe most of the ideas in the following section to my reading of various works by Stanley Hauerwas.
11. Hauerwas, *Vision and Virtue*, p. 29.
12. Hauerwas, *Character and the Christian Life*, p. 223.
13. Ibid., pp. 179–233.

14. Hauerwas, *Character and the Christian Life*, p. 223.

15. Hauerwas, *A Community of Character*, p. 144.

16. James Loder, *The Transforming Moment* (San Francisco: Harper & Row, 1981).

17. H. Richard Niebuhr, *The Meaning of Revelation*, p. 133.

18. See Brueggemann's discussion and critique of faith development theory. Walter Brueggemann, "The Exodus Narrative as Israel's Articulation of Faith Development," *Hope within History*, chapter 1.

8. Church: An Ecology of Spiritual Care and Formation

1. Dietrich Bonhoeffer, *Spiritual Care*, trans. Jay C. Rochelle (Philadelphia: Fortress Press, 1985), p. 38.

2. This chart was inspired by Damien Isabell. See *The Spiritual Director: A Practical Guide* (Chicago: Franciscan Herald Press, 1976).

3. Howard Grimes, *The Church Redemptive*, p. 103.

4. Cf. Tom Oden, *Care of Souls in the Classic Tradition* (Philadelphia: Fortress Press, 1984).

5. Bonhoeffer, *Spiritual Care*, p. 32.

6. Ibid., p. 36.

7. Ibid., p. 35.

8. Elliot W. Eisner, *The Educational Imagination: On the Design and Evaluation of School Programs*, rev. ed. (New York: Macmillan, 1979).

9. John Dewey, no source cited, as quoted by Eisner, *The Educational Imagination*, p. 74.

10. Foster, *Celebration*, p. 48.

11. James Smart, *The Strange Silence of the Bible in the Church: A Study in Hermeneutics* (Philadelphia: Westminster Press, 1970).

9. Christian Education for Formation

1. My thanks to Richard Osmer, Union Theological Seminary at Richmond, Va., for helping me to think about these issues through his unpublished paper "The Teaching Office of the Church: The Contribution of Luther and Calvin," delivered to the United

Methodist Association of Professors of Chrisitan Education, Estes Park, Colorado, August 1988.

2. See Peter Berger, *The Heretical Imperative: Contemporary Possibilities of Religious Affirmation* (Garden City, N.Y.: Anchor Press/Doubleday, 1980), p. 57.

3. For an excellent essay on the nature of teaching in a Christian context, see Charles R. Foster, *Teaching in the Community of Faith* (Nashville: Abingdon Press, 1983).

4. Edward L. Thorndike, "The Contribution of Psychology to Education," *Journal of Educational Psychology*, 1910, quoted in Eisner, *The Educational Imagination*, p. 6.

5. See Parker J. Palmer, *To Know As We Are Known: A Spirituality of Education* (San Francisco: Harper & Row, 1983). I am indebted to Palmer's discussion for some of the insights in this section.

6. Ibid. See especially chap. 5, entitled "To Teach Is to Create a Space . . ." and chap. 6, ". . . In which Obedience to Truth is Practiced."

7. D. Campbell Wyckoff, *Theory and Design of the Christian Education Curriculum* (Philadelphia: Westminster Press, 1961), p. 58.

8. As Ted Peters points out, dialogue derives from the Greek word *logos* for "word" or "conversation," and the prefix is *dia*, not *di* as we commonly think. *Dia* is a Greek preposition meaning "through" or "throughout." Dialogue means we converse in order to draw out the full meaning and significance of a subject in order to discern the truth together. See Ted Peters, "A Christian Theology of Interreligious Dialogue," *Christian Century* (October 15, 1986): 883.

9. Søren Kierkegaard, *Concluding Unscientific Postscript*, trans. David Swenson and Walter Lowrie (Princeton: Princeton University Press, 1941), p. 42.

10. Ibid. p. 51.

11. Robert W. Hovda, "Hope for the Future: A Summary," in *Made, Not Born: New Perspectives on Christian Initiation and the Catechumenate* (Notre Dame, Ind.: University of Notre Dame Press, The Murphy Center for Liturgical Research, 1976), p. 154.

12. These learning tasks are based upon the work of D. Campbell

Wyckoff, *Theory and Design*, passim. This book is still a *must* in educational theory and practice!

13. See George Lindbeck, *The Nature of Doctrine.*
14. Ibid., p. 34.
15. Ibid., p. 35.
16. Søren Kierkegaard, *On Authority and Revelation*, trans. W. Lowrie (Princeton: Princeton University Press, 1955), pp. 168-69. I discovered this quote in Fred Craddock, *Overhearing the Gospel*, p. 60.
17. Geertz, "Religion as a Cultural System," p. 665.
18. Beverly Wildung Harrison, *Making the Connections: Essays in Feminist Social Ethic.* ed. Carol Robb. (Boston: Beacon Press, 1985). This section on shared praxis owes substantially to Harrison's chapter entitled "Theological Reflection in the Struggle for Liberation: A Feminist Perspective."
19. Ibid., p. 259.
20. Ibid., p. 253.
21. Ibid., p. 260.
22. Carlos Mesters, "The Use of the Bible in Christian Communities of the Common People," chap. 16 in *The Challenge of Basic Christian Communities: Papers from the International Ecumenical Congress of Theology, Sao Paul, Brazil, 1980* (Maryknoll, N.Y.: Orbis Press, 1981), pp. 197-210.
23. See Craig Dykstra, "Under Certain Conditions: The Church's Educational Ministry" (The 1988 Bradner Lecture Series) *Virginia Seminary Journal* 39, no. 3 (June 1988): 2-11.
24. This tension is present in both secular and religious education. In *Experience and Education* (1938), John Dewey lamented the dichotomy between content-based (traditional) and experience-based (progressive) education. Dewey was disturbed that his experiential approach was miscontrued by those on both sides of the debate; he was critical of the progressives as well as the traditionalists.

Epilogue

1. Craddock, *Overhearing the Gospel*, p. 79.
2. Ibid., p. 65.